MEN

WITH

Great Explorers of the North American West

SAND

JOHN MORING

TWODOT

A · TWODOT · BOOK

Falcon® Publishing is continually expanding its list of regional history books. You can order extra copies of this book and get information and prices for other Falcon books by writing to Falcon, P.O. Box 1718, Helena, MT 59624 or calling 1-800-582-2665. Also, please ask for a free copy of our current catalog listing all Falcon books. To contact us via e-mail, visit our home page at http://www.falconguide.com

©1998 John Moring.
TwoDot is an imprint of Falcon® Publishing, Inc., Helena, Montana.
Design, typesetting, and other prepress work by Falcon Publishing, Helena, Montana.

Cover photos: (top right) USS Vincennes, U.S. Navy (detail)/Courtesy, Peabody Essex Museum, Salem, MA. (bottom) "The Rendezvous" by Alfred Jacob Miller/Courtesy, American Heritage Center, University of Wyoming.

Printed in the United States of America.

Library of Congress Cataloging-in-Publication Data

Moring, John, 1946-
    Men with sand: great explorers of the North American West / John Moring.
        p.   cm.
    Includes bibliograhical references and index.
    Contents: Introduction: the great explorers—Alexander Mackenzie—Lewis and
    Clark—John Colter—Manuel Lisa—Zebulon Pike—Stephen Long—Jedediah
Smith—The Patties—Charles Wilkes—John C. Frémont—John Wesley Powell.
        ISBN 1-56044-620-X
        1. Explorers—West (U.S.)—Biography. 2. West (U.S.)—Discovery and
    exploration—American. I. Title.
    F592.M73   1998
    978'.02'0922—dc21
        [B]   97-43468
                                                                        CIP

The Publisher gratefully acknowledges the assistance of Dr. Harry Fritz, Professor of History, University of Montana, Missoula, Montana.

Contents

The Great Explorers

*A*t the end of the eighteenth century, much of western North America remained unexplored. No one even knew how far it was from the eastern centers of population to the West Coast.

Almost three hundred years earlier, when Columbus landed in Panama during his fourth voyage, he didn't cross the relatively narrow strip of land that separated the two great oceans. In 1513, when Spanish explorer Vasco Nuñez de Balboa stood on a high point of ground in Central America and saw the Pacific Ocean, he realized he was standing on a new continent, one that was quite narrow—at least at that latitude.

Later Spanish explorers crisscrossed Mexico and the Southwest and eventually concluded that the continent was wider that far north. North of Mexico, the interior was virtually unknown except to Native Americans; and beyond their traditional territories, Native Americans had only a limited geographical knowledge.

In the late eighteenth century, a few fur traders and trappers had ventured into the interior as far west as northern Alberta. The trappers heard about a large mountain range—the Rocky Mountains—that ran north–south. No one had any concept of how high or how wide the range was. Were these mountains like the Alleghenies and Appalachians, or were they something more formidable? Were there broad passes through the Rockies where great rivers flowed? Was there a "Northwest Passage," a new trade route from the Atlantic to the Pacific?

For years, British explorers—Cook, Vancouver, and others—and the adventuresome Spanish had been poking into the bays and inlets along the Pacific Coast, mapping headlands and potential ports. Even American merchant ships had traveled these waters. But the interior of the West remained a question.

It took a special breed of men to provide the answers. Imagine what it took for Alexander Mackenzie and his men to pull a canoe up the side of a mountain; or for John Colter to outrun a band of Blackfeet Indians, then plunge into an icy river; or for Jedediah Smith to help sew his own scalp back on his head after an attack by a grizzly bear; or for John Wesley Powell to survive the Colorado River's most dangerous rapids. Such men were said to "have sand" or to "have sand in their craw." The terms are old, but they accurately describe the special daring and talents those early western explorers needed in order to survive.

These famous men had very special talents; but they weren't the only men with sand. We often remember the leaders of important expeditions and forget those who traveled with them. Everyone has heard of Meriwether Lewis and William Clark, but most of us do not recognize the name of George Drouillard, who traveled every mile with the two explorers and later did more exploring with fur trader Manuel Lisa. We remember the man who conquered the Colorado River, John Wesley Powell. But the one-armed Powell, despite his grit and determination, could never have rowed a boat by himself. He needed other men of equal resolve to help him complete his journey.

Singling out a few explorers as "men with sand" implies that these men were a cut above their traveling companions, which is far from the truth. Jedediah Smith, Zebulon Pike, John Colter, and Stephen Long represent many others who slogged through mud, hauled canoes over mountaintops, struggled from one desert waterhole to the next, and suffered innumerable other hardships alongside their more famous leaders. The stories of the famous explorers are really the stories of a much larger group of rugged individuals—which, incidentally, included a few women, such as Sacagawea and Emma Dean Powell.

The expedition leaders became famous—which does not mean they were perfect. Most were not beloved by the men in their companies. Zebulon Pike, Charles Wilkes, and John C. Frémont were all brought up before courts martial (two of them for political reasons). Charles Wilkes's achievements were incredible, yet he was thoroughly despised by most of the men who served under him. Manuel Lisa, consumed by business success, drove his employees relentlessly. He fought with them and came to fear for his life around them, but he never let personal differences interfere with achieving his objectives. John C. Frémont, a nineteenth-century George S. Patton, had an ego to match his bravado. Many of his men ridiculed him, yet even his most vocal detractor, cartographer Charles Preuss, signed on to accompany "the Pathfinder" on expedition after expedition. True men with sand were often complex individuals. What they all had in common was a special ability to succeed. Their legacies were in their accomplishments.

Even the terms "explorer" and "discover" are misnomers. The western explorers of the late eighteenth to mid-nineteenth centuries really only visited lands unfamiliar to those living in eastern North America. Native American tribes had been living in these "undiscovered" reaches for centuries. They knew about the beaver and buffalo, the rivers and mountains—at least in their immediate geographic regions. The people we call explorers traveled far enough and crossed enough barriers to see a bigger picture; they mapped or documented large areas of land. Their documents paved the way for the westward expansion of the white population, and for what we have called progress.

Settlers in the United States and eastern Canada commonly thought of Native Americans in generic terms. They were an undeveloped race with a radically different lifestyle and different customs from those living in so-called civilized areas of the East. Meriwether Lewis and William Clark proved some errors in Easterners' generalizations.

Along with President Thomas Jefferson, Lewis and Clark had a strong respect for and curiosity about Native Americans. Lewis and Clark diligently described their impressions of the fifty-some tribes they met along their route. Their journals are filled with records of the culture shocks they experienced when encountering some of the local customs. Under Presidential orders, they were to establish good relations with these tribes, and they were remarkably successful. Only one tragic incident with the Blackfeet darkened that record.

Lewis and Clark admired the Nez Percé and many of the Plains tribes, but they thought less highly of some other tribes. The explorers' dislikes influenced readers' opinions of such tribes, whose cultures were more difficult to know and understand. In attempting to tell the stories of the men with sand, this problem is chronic: we usually only have one side of the story.

Several of the explorers—Jedediah Smith, Meriwether Lewis,

Sylvester and James Pattie, John Colter, and John Wesley Powell—either killed Native Americans or had their companions die at the hands of tribal warriors. (Charles Wilkes had tragic encounters with South Seas natives rather than Native Americans.) These experiences probably encouraged a bias. And only the journals, letters, and accounts of the white explorers remain for us to study. In some cases, accounts were verified by others, either white or Native American. We should keep in mind that the stories of many of the men are their versions of exploration and encounters with people of quite different cultures.

Some of the explorers' accounts may have even had hidden agendas. James Pattie was an avowed Indian-hater; he especially hated the Apaches. His many descriptions of Indian torture, mutilation, and other atrocities may have been embellished in order to justify his own overly offensive acts. Perhaps it is true that the last survivor can rewrite history. We have only spotty evidence against James Pattie's reports. We know he wasn't always accurate: some incidents he wrote about in the first person happened to people other than himself. Other incidents he documented may really have occurred—similar behavior (for example, Apache atrocities) was recorded by others. Maybe James Pattie wanted to treat his readers to a ripping good story along with the real events in his life. We will never know the complete truth. We don't have the Umpqua version of that tribe's attack on Jedediah Smith's party in Oregon, or the Blackfeet version of their tragic zencounter with Meriwether Lewis and his men.

On the other hand, many western explorers candidly recounted the positive aspects of their encounters with Native Americans. Jedediah Smith, who fought the Arikara, Comanche, Mojave, Umpqua, and others, readily acknowledged that his life had been saved by the kindness of other tribes in California, Oregon, and elsewhere.

Captain John Bell, leading a detachment of Major Stephen Long's command, credited the kindness of a passing band of Osage warriors with saving his men from starvation. Lewis and Clark recognized the Nez Percé for saving their lives when they were lost in a mountain snowstorm. On the surface, the deaths of some of John Wesley Powell's men at the hands of a village of Shivwits seems a hostile act. But Powell made certain to present the tribe's honest explanation of the tragedy as one of mistaken identity.

The exploration of the West often involved a clash of cultures. Most western explorers considered the theft of axes, food, furs, or horses amoral; yet, such practices were widespread among many tribes, and had been a fact of life in relations between tribes for centuries. The explorers, having grown up in a particular tradition, and later, exploring under conditions of great hardship, could not describe certain events in neutral terms.

The journals and other supporting documents of the men with sand may present a one-sided impression of Native Americans. They cannot provide a complete history. But they at least attempted to describe fascinating encounters between people who lived in the West and those who dared to travel amongst them.

Where others would have turned back, the men with sand pressed on. While others only talked, the men with sand acted. When others would have been satisfied with the ordinary, the men with sand often did the extraordinary. ■

CHAPTER ONE

~ *Across Canada*

Alexander Mackenzie

*L*eaning over the side of his canoe, the twenty-five-year-old explorer dipped his hand in the water. It was frigid, as it had been throughout much of the long journey. He cupped his hand, brought a mouthful to his lips, and took a sip.

The water was salty.

Alexander Mackenzie's heart skipped a beat. The broad expanse ahead must be sea water. Could this be the dreamed-of Northwest Passage—a route from civilization to the Pacific coast and the trade markets of Asia beyond? Mackenzie shouted to his companions. He pointed ahead at what had appeared to be a large lake.

The men dug their paddles into the water and propelled the large canoe more quickly downstream. A large tidal area of what appeared to be a shoreless lake opened up before them.

As the explorers got closer, they saw something strange: the surface of the water was covered with ice. Something was very wrong.

~ ~ ~

It was Peter Pond, a fifty-year-old trader from Connecticut, who had given Alexander Mackenzie the notion to search for the North-west Passage. Pond described his theory of a watery passage westward to anyone who would listen. If such a path existed, its discovery could simplify the trade route from the populated cities of Europe, the eastern United States, and Canada to the rich regions of the Pacific.

The same dream had been pursued for hundreds of years by hundreds of explorers and visionaries. Ever since Columbus tried to find a westward route to Asia and stumbled across an unknown land mass in the way, people had tried to find an easy passage from the Atlantic coast of that land mass to its Pacific coast.

Pond was a principal in the North West Company, a fur-trading enterprise that had outposts strung from eastern Canada and Detroit to what is now northern Alberta. Pond himself manned one of them. He had been quite an explorer in his younger days. The first white man to venture into the interior of northwestern Canada, he had discovered Lake Athabaska and the Athabaska River.

Ever since his arrival in the wilds of western Canada, Pond had heard stories about a water-passage to the Pacific Ocean. Indians visiting his remote trading post brought stories about a river that flowed west into saltwater. The more Pond heard, the more convinced he became: there had to be a Northwest Passage.

Unfortunately, most people tired of Peter Pond's stories. His past was somewhat checkered, and his enthusiasm exceeded any hard evidence.

But one man listened: a young Scottish trader named Alexander Mackenzie. Born in 1764 on the island of Lewis in the Outer Hebrides, Mackenzie moved with his family to New York when he was ten. During the American Revolution, his father joined the British Army, and the boy was sent to Montreal.

After some schooling, Mackenzie joined the XY Company, a relatively small fur company and a competitor of the larger North West Company, which was fast becoming a dominant force in the fur business. When the XY Company sent Mackenzie to Detroit and farther west, the competition was thoroughly impressed with the young Scot's leadership skills. Mackenzie was only twenty-three at the time, but the North West Company made him a full partner and sent him to the wild country of Lake Athabaska.

There Mackenzie met Peter Pond and listened to the man's stories. While he worked for his company, building Fort Chipewyan along the shores of Lake Athabaska, Mackenzie was preoccupied with a dream of searching for the Northwest Passage. His best chance, Mackenzie reasoned, was a large river that flowed westward out of Great Slave Lake, located north of Fort Chipewyan. Such a river might cut a path through the Rocky Mountains and flow down to the sea.

On June 3, 1789, Mackenzie got a chance to prove his theory. He convinced the North West Company of the potential benefits of westward exploration, and as a full partner, he was given leave and the means to go. With five men and two of their Indian wives in one canoe, and several other Indians in other canoes, Mackenzie headed for Great Slave Lake. The party crossed Lake Athabaska and spent a week traveling down the Slave River. It rained often and the mosquitoes were thick, but the traveling itself was not overly difficult. The party did have to negotiate rapids, portaging its loads around the worst ones, as well as around the shallow spots. So it went—paddle, portage, paddle, portage, forty to eighty miles each day. The explorers shot and ate ducks, geese, and beavers along the way.

At last the group arrived at Great Slave Lake, a huge, three-hundred-mile-long expanse of water. Storms were mixing the lake into a froth. The explorers met with waves higher than their canoes and were

SIR ALEXANDER MACKENZIE
National Gallery of Canada, Ottowa

pummeled by chunks of ice still bobbing on the water's surface. The canoes managed to reach the western shore and find the large, unknown river that flowed westward. From this point on, the land was uncharted. Undaunted, Alexander Mackenzie headed the canoes downstream.

The explorers now met with very different terrain. Vast forests gave way to bleak, barren plains. The party pushed on, traveling three hundred miles before they spotted the huge Rocky Mountains rising in the distance.

As they paddled closer to the mountains, Mackenzie's spirits rose. Would his chosen waterway cut a path through the great range and flow into the sea? In answer to his question, the river slowly turned northward, running parallel to the steep slopes.

By now the river was huge. Rainfall and snowmelt had added to its size and strength. Each new tributary they passed increased the river's width. The canoes were carried downstream at a relentless pace.

Days became weeks. The men called on their leader to abandon his vision and return home. Tribes they encountered along the way were more and more hostile and suspicious; the interlopers were justifiably afraid. But Mackenzie urged them on.

Almost six weeks after the party had left Lake Athabaska, the river finally slowed its pace, then split into three channels. Mackenzie was confused, but he ordered the canoes into the middle channel. Soon they saw what appeared to be a huge lake in the distance.

Here, Mackenzie dipped his hand in and was elated to taste the water's saltiness. Soon thereafter, the party saw the ice. Only around the edges of the land was the water clear of it. Mackenzie's heart sank. He realized that their journey of more than a thousand miles had taken them not to the Pacific Ocean, but to the Arctic Ocean. The route was useless as a Northwest Passage. Others who had attempted to travel great rivers from Canada's east had reached the same conclusion—every waterway ended in the icy Arctic.

Mackenzie and his party explored the bay of the great river for five days, even chasing a beluga whale at one point. But they knew their trip had been in vain. They still had to make the thousand-mile return journey—this time, upstream.

Mackenzie named the river Disappointment. The explorers set out to retrace their route back to Fort Chipewyan. It was no small feat, especially against the strong current. To add to their problems, they were at the extreme northern reaches of the earth; daylight hours were rapidly declining as autumn approached. The countryside would soon be in darkness throughout most of each day. Despite the hardships, the travelers reached Fort Chipewyan just before the long winter arrived.

Though Mackenzie didn't know it at the time, his trip represented no small achievement. The river he had named Disappointment is one of the longest rivers in North America. It was later renamed the Mackenzie River, after the man who first traveled its length.

Mackenzie's exploits were far from ended. He hadn't given up on his dream of a Northwest Passage. His most famous expedition was still ahead of him.

When Mackenzie returned, his partners in the North West Company were not pleased with him. He had spent valuable time and too much money on his search for a Northwest Passage; he had ended up in the Arctic Ocean, surrounded by barren countryside; and he had not a single fur to show for his efforts. To make amends, Mackenzie redoubled his fur-trading efforts at Fort Chipewyan and pushed his dreams to the back of his mind.

But Mackenzie knew that he if he was going to try again, he would need to learn more about celestial navigation. After two more years in the wilderness, he took a load of furs back to Montreal and boarded a ship for England.

In England, Mackenzie examined the maps and journals of Jonathan Carver, James Cook, and other explorers of the Northwest. He pored over their maps in detail and learned to use the most up-to-date navigational instruments. In April 1792, he returned to Montreal and convinced the North West Company that he had found another viable option for travel to the Pacific Coast: the Peace River.

The Peace River was familiar to Alexander Mackenzie and other settlers in the Lake Athabaska area. Its mouth was near Fort Chipewyan; the huge river's source was in the unknown west.

Alexander Mackenzie's cousin and others were sent three hundred miles up the Peace River to build a small fort. Mackenzie traveled upriver to the fort in the winter of 1793. Even at that distance from its mouth, the river continued to point westward, unlike the ill-fated Disappointment River. Mackenzie was convinced that this was the route to the Pacific. On April 25, 1793, when the ice finally broke on the river, he sent six canoes back to Fort Chipewyan to prepare for another expedition.

This time, Mackenzie was accompanied by six voyageurs (the trapper-trader-explorers of the northern waters), a clerk (Alexander McKay), two Indian guides and hunters, one dog, and three thousand pounds of food and other gear—all in one twenty-five-foot birch-bark canoe.

The expedition began on May 9, 1793. The first week of travel was familiar and easy. In high spirits, the explorers continued westward and spotted the Rocky Mountains in the distance on May 17.

Two days later the trip turned dangerous. The party entered the Peace River Canyon—twenty miles of vicious rapids edged by sheer cliffs, some a thousand feet high. For two days, the men lived a constant hell. With no rest, they poled and towed the canoe around each curve of the river, terrified of what new danger they might find. Chunks of rock dropped on them from the cliffs. Snags poked holes in the canoe, forcing the men to find some tenuous perch along the rock cliff in order to stop and patch the holes. When they could, the travelers unloaded the canoe and portaged their way around some of North America's most difficult waters.

Two days and a night of constant effort seemed to get them nowhere. Unsure of how many miles of rapids were ahead, Mackenzie saw only two options: abandon the trip, admit failure, and turn back; or try something that few people would even consider. He made his decision. Using hatchets and axes, the men cut a path through a forested part of the river's steep bank. It took them days to get from the river to the top of the canyon. They then used ropes to drag the huge canoe and their supplies up the hillside to the top of the ridge.

At the top at last, the party found themselves in a huge briar patch that had grown over an old burn. They spent days more cutting their way through it. Dragging the canoe, foot by foot, they paralleled the path of the river far below.

Finally, on May 24, 1793, the explorers looked at the ribbon of water below and saw only quiet stretches—no more rapids. Cutting another path down the hillside, the party reentered the Peace River.

Another week went by; then the river forked. The lay of the land was now well beyond the knowledge of the Native American guides, but Mackenzie remembered the words of an old Native American who had visited Fort Chipewyan before their trip. Not knowing whether the old man had been right or wrong, Mackenzie directed the canoe

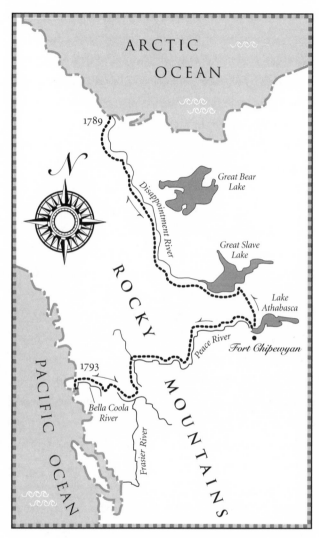

~ Mackenzie's route from Lake Athabasca
north to the Arctic Ocean.

~ Mackenzie's route from Lake Athabasca
south and west to the Pacific Ocean.

into the left-hand, or southern branch, now known as the Parsnip. Mackenzie's companions were not pleased. The southern branch looked like the worst choice: it was deep and narrow, and certainly not a shoe-in for a Northwest Passage. But with the confidence of a true leader, Mackenzie pursuaded the others to continue.

For many difficult miles, it seemed the men would prove their leader wrong. The river narrowed even further. By the time the party reached the headwaters, Mackenzie was scanning the shorelines, hoping local Indians might appear and offer directions.

On June 9, when forward progress had all but halted, Mackenzie's prayers were answered. Along the shoreline, watching the explorers and their canoe, stood three men, three women, and six children. All were short and round-faced, and the women's faces were striped with paint.

The Indians stood motionless, in awe of the strangers. They had heard of white men, but had never seen one. Yet their spears were iron-tipped, a sign to the explorers that these people had had contact with Europeans. The Indians explained to the guides that the spear tips came from the west. The village where they had traded for the iron points was an eighteen-day walk away. Those other Indians had in turn acquired the metal from another tribe even farther to the west.

The explorers' morale crumbled. After a month of extremely difficult travel, their goal was still very distant. Not only were they in the middle of nowhere, but if the Indians were correct, no true Northwest Passage existed here.

Mackenzie managed to find a ray of hope. Though the Indians had told his interpreters that no rivers flowed westward, they knew of a river that flowed southward. Maybe this river would enter the great Columbia, which led to the sea.

Mackenzie engaged one of the Indians as a guide. The men

portaged their canoe a short distance between two small lakes and reached a south-flowing river. They now seemed headed in the right direction, but travel was far from easy. Shallow gravel bars crossed the small river again and again. The men had to stop at each one, wade into the water, and pull their canoe across. In many places, fallen trees blocked their passage; these had to be chopped away before travel could continue.

Then, what had been only difficult became dangerous. Rounding a bend, the voyagers found themselves amongst violent rapids. In the foaming water, the canoe lurched to one side and capsized. The current swept the men downstream through more rapids and knocked them against jagged rocks that jutted up through the water. They were only saved by a crosscurrent that caught them and pulled them into shallow water. They scrambled ashore.

Of all the low points of the trip, this was surely the lowest. The canoe was washed ashore too, but most of the ammunition and much of the food was lost. Mackenzie's men demanded that he abandon the quest for a westward passage so that they could return home.

Alexander Mackenzie showed his leadership again by rallying his followers. He broke out some of the remaining food and the rest of the rum. Somewhat sated, the men agreed to patch the canoe and continue on. But the oilcloth, bark, and gum of the canoe's many patches began to weigh it down. Two men could no longer lift it. Mackenzie wondered how long the canoe could stay afloat and how the inevitable future holes could be patched.

The men set off down the river, deciding to call it the Bad River. The name reflected not only their catastrophe in the rapids but the general misery of a journey plagued by mosquitoes and oozy mud. When their canoe entered a larger river (now known as the Fraser River), Mackenzie phonetically recorded its Indian name, "Tacouchetessé." The brown waters carved a route through dense forests, and the party pressed onward.

Several days later, as the group passed through what is now known as Fort George Canyon, they received another blow: their Indian guide deserted in the night. Mackenzie hoped to find another, but the few wooden structures they found along the shore were abandoned.

Finally, around a bend, they encountered a group of Carrier Indians. The tribe, equally surprised to see a group of white men in a canoe approaching their village, panicked and started firing arrows at the strangers. It was a tense moment that could have put an abrupt end to the historic trek. Mackenzie ordered one of his hunters to cover him while he waded ashore alone. His show of bravado impressed the Indians, and when he started handing out mirrors and beads as presents, the hostility evaporated.

The Indian interpreters who had accompanied the travelers from Lake Athabaska attempted to communicate with the Carriers but without much success. Through hand signs and similar words, they managed to understand one thing: hostile tribes lived downriver. But Alexander Mackenzie would heed none of their warnings. Whether brave, bull-headed, or both, he directed the canoe downstream. Other tribes they met warned him of the same thing, but he kept moving downriver.

The expedition had other worries: the traveling became slow and difficult and the supplies were almost gone. The remaining food had to be rationed. Hostile Indians now seemed the least of their troubles. The Northwest Passage became an impossible dream to all of them. Alexander Mackenzie just hoped to complete his journey and reach the sea. But this river would not even help him do that.

Ordering a retreat for the first time, Mackenzie returned to the Carrier village. He found it deserted. The Carriers, apparently surprised again by the reappearance of the explorers, had disappeared into the forest.

Once again, the twenty-nine-year-old Mackenzie had to rouse his men from despair. Somehow, he convinced them to build another canoe. In their new vessel, they traveled up a small tributary stream—the Blackwater—and arrived at its headwaters on July 4. Here the expedition abandoned its attempts at water travel. The men hid the canoe, a keg of gunpowder, and some of the remaining food. Whatever the distance to the sea, they would cross it on foot.

Each man carried a load of about ninety pounds, along with a rifle and ammunition. The explorers trekked over a mountain pass, through forests, and across streams; they averaged fifteen to thirty miles a day through almost constant rain.

Just when their strength and endurance seemed gone, the weary travelers stumbled into a large Indian village along the lower Bella Coola River. In one of those fortunate events that seem to bless every great adventure, the Bella Coolas befriended the explorers, filling their stomachs with salmon taken from elaborate weirs. More importantly, the Bella Coolas agreed to guide the men downriver in their own canoes.

The party still had some distance to travel on the Bella Coola. Near its mouth, the stream split into several channels. The downriver tribes were quite hostile. When one of the party's axes was stolen, a near-incident occurred. Mackenzie demanded the axe be returned. It was.

Finally, on July 20, 1793, seventy-three days after leaving Fort Chipewyan, Alexander Mackenzie borrowed a larger canoe from a coastal tribe and paddled with his men into saltwater.

It was a crowning achievement: Mackenzie's party was the first to cross the North American continent north of Mexico. Mackenzie noted the event in his journal:

"Twenty pounds weight of pemmican, fifteen pounds of rice, and six pounds of flour among ten half-starved men, in a leaky vessel, and on a barbarous coast."

For Mackenzie, the coast's barbarism lay partly in its weather: constant rain and high winds buffeted the canoe. And, local tribes continued to harass the explorers. Canoe loads of Indians followed them, taunting and yelling. One group was still irritated about an incident with another ship's crew (it may have been explorer George Vancouver and his crew, who, it turns out, had visited the area some months before; Vancouver's journal doesn't mention any incident). The Indians followed Mackenzie ashore and tried to steal anything they could. They took some things but eventually left the explorers alone.

Doing their best to ignore the hostilities, the explorers spent two days making careful celestial measurements, so as to pinpoint their achievement for the world. Mackenzie obtained some melted grease and vermilion from a local village and painted the following message on a large rock:

"Alexander Mackenzie, from Canada, by land, the Twenty-second of July, One-Thousand Seven Hundred and Ninety-Three."

∾ ∾ ∾

Mackenzie's return trip was not without incident. Rapids, rain, and mosquitoes plagued the group the entire way, and the early days were filled with encounters with hostile tribes. But homeward travel is always much more rapid. The explorers paddled across Lake Athabaska only a month after leaving the coast.

Alexander Mackenzie's achievements went unappreciated for

years. He returned to fur trading, but after the partners of the North West Company had a falling out, he quit and went to England.

Mackenzie's dream of a Northwest Passage was not extinguished. He tried to convince the Colonial Secretary, Lord Hobart, that the Saskatchewan River might flow westward and would be worth exploring. But no one seemed interested.

In 1801 Mackenzie published the accounts of his two treks in a volume entitled *Voyages From Montreal*. The book gained popularity in England and North America, and it led the British Government to recognize the amazing accomplishments of this adventuresome Scot. In January 1802, Alexander Mackenzie was knighted by King George. The notoriety achieved by his book, the fortune accumulated from his years in the fur trade, and his knighthood made him famous for the rest of his life.

Of all his achievements, perhaps his most important was the effect of the epilogue of his book on one avid reader. In it, he urged the British to "secure the trade of furs and other resources." The reader, Thomas Jefferson of the United States, saw this as a warning that the British would lay claim to much of the Northwest unless the United States got there first. Jefferson made sure to show a copy to his secretary, Meriwether Lewis. ■

CHAPTER TWO

~ *The Great Expedition*

Lewis and Clark

eriwether Lewis always took things seriously. When President Thomas Jefferson gave him a list of instructions for an expedition up the Missouri River, Lewis determined to carry out every one that he could.

The President asked the explorers to record, among other things, the "mineral productions of every kind; but more particularly metals, limestone, pit coal & saltpetre; salines & mineral waters, noting the temperature of the last, & such circumstances as may indicate their character." So, when members of the Lewis and Clark Expedition spotted an unusual rock outcropping along the Missouri River in August 1804, Lewis went to investigate.

The bluff along the river showed evidence of several kinds of minerals. Instead of just collecting samples, Lewis pounded the different materials into powder. He sniffed them, tasted them—and then became violently ill.

According to his co-leader, William Clark, Lewis had taken President Jefferson's instructions a little too literally. He had sampled deposits of copper, cobalt, pyrite, alum—and arsenic.

～ ～ ～

When Jefferson began to plan for an expedition across the North American continent, and wondered who could carry out such a difficult task, he immediately thought of his friend and former neighbor, Meriwether Lewis. Lewis had all the qualities of an ideal candidate. He was young, had lived in rural areas, and was an experienced Army officer. He also knew something of the customs and manners of eastern Indian tribes and had fought in various Indian wars.

In addition, Lewis had a strong scientific curiosity. He was interested in everything from plants and animals to rocks and fossils. He knew something of medicine—at least, of the folk remedies of the day. Most importantly, Meriwether Lewis was completely honest and trustworthy.

Jefferson was an amateur scientist in his own right; maybe he saw a little of himself in Lewis. What prompted the third President of the United States to mount an expedition across the continent was more than scientific curiosity, however. His desire had a history to it.

Jefferson had tried several times to send small groups of men westward. None of them ever got far. Some of the land to the west clearly belonged to either France, Spain, or Great Britain. The rest was a confusing mixture of claims. Any expedition sent by the young United States could easily encounter problems with one of the other countries.

That changed in 1803. Spain had ceded a large part of western North America to France—a roughly triangular tract of land extending from New Orleans northward across the vast Great Plains, up the Missouri River, to the Continental Divide. Napoleon Bonaparte had intended to expand the French empire into the Western Hemisphere. But a war with Great Britain was on the French horizon, and

Napoleon needed money. As a lucky consequence, he offered this tremendous tract of land to the United States for the sum of $15 million, or about three cents per acre.

Jefferson was amazed at the offer. At the time, $15 million was a great deal of money. Jefferson also questioned the constitutionality of his accepting such a sale on his own, as president. Still, Napoleon's offer was one he could not turn down. After agonizing over the decision for several months, the President signed the purchase agreement. The size of the United States doubled overnight.

The young nation now had every right to explore its western reaches. The President was intensely curious about the land—its wildlife and geography, its inhabitants and their customs. Jefferson wanted to develop peaceful relations with the Native American tribes of the area and to open up trade with them. And he wanted to develop and dominate the fur trade of the upper Missouri River. This would not only allow the United States to compete with the British Hudson's Bay Company, but would also keep the British farther to the north.

Jefferson was a visionary. He knew that the population of the United States would grow, and that westward settlement was inevitable. He wanted to know what was out there, and he conceived the idea of a Corps of Discovery. The commission was too large even for a man of Meriwether Lewis's talents. Jefferson suggested seeking a second officer, and Lewis immediately chose William Clark, a former Army captain who had previously been Lewis's commander.

Clark, the younger brother of the famous soldier George Rogers Clark, was also well qualified for the task at hand. The red-haired Clark was outgoing and friendly, and the perfect complement to Meriwether Lewis. Clark readily accepted the assignment.

Lewis wanted Clark and himself, as leaders of the expedition, to be equal in rank. Lewis was an Army captain, as Clark had been

MERIWETHER LEWIS
PAINTING BY CHARLES WILLSON PEALE C.1807
Independence National Historic Park

WILLIAM CLARK
PAINTING BY CHARLES WILLSON PEALE C.1810
Independence National Historic Park

before he left the Army some years earlier. The President agreed to the request and sent in the orders, but War Department red tape changed Clark's appointment from captain to second lieutenant. Lewis was angry, but the military held firm. So, Lewis simply informed everyone that his friend William Clark was a captain, equal in rank and equal in responsibility. The matter was never questioned again.

Preparations for the trip actually began before the President finalized the Louisiana Purchase. Lewis and Clark spent many hours assembling supplies for the trip and selecting the men who would accompany them. These were no simple tasks. The two men knew something about the upper Missouri River but little about the rest of their intended route. They had no idea how long the trip would take or what they might encounter along the way.

The supply list covered many pages and included such things as 2,800 fish hooks; 48 calico shirts (as gifts for Indian tribes); chronometers, protractors, and quadrants; flints and powder; flannel shirts, blankets, and numerous other items for their own use—all properly itemized. Lewis estimated that the expedition would cost $2,500. The calico shirts and other presents for the Indians they would encounter made up the largest single expense, but the two leaders also included $87 for "contingencies."

Lewis and Clark did not take the choice of their fellow travelers lightly either. After all, they might be in close quarters together for many months. The men would have to be able to follow orders, tolerate each other, and weather unknown hardships.

Eventually, Lewis and Clark settled on the forty-one men who would accompany them. Other guides—Indian and French-Canadian—joined them for portions of the journey; a few of the soldiers left the expedition in its early weeks. Thirty-two men (plus Sacagawea and her young son) would cross the Rocky Mountains with the explorers. Two other important members of the expedition were Clark's slave, York, and Lewis's Newfoundland dog, Seaman. York amazed many of the Native Americans with his size, strength, and skin color. Indian women were especially curious about him. Seaman often captured and retrieved small animals—many of which were preserved and returned to the East for scientific study.

Jefferson's major objectives for the expedition were the mapping and exploration of the new territories (paving the way for fur traders and settlers) and scientific discovery. In April and May of 1803, Jefferson sent Meriwether Lewis to Philadelphia to train with some of the nation's most respected scientists. Lewis learned about navigation from mathematician Robert Patterson; about the observation of nature from Benjamin Smith Barton; and about accurate measurement and observation of the plants and animals that the expedition might encounter from anatomist Caspar Wistar. Lewis even went to Big Bone Lick, a dig site near Cincinnati, to excavate dinosaur bones with a local paleontologist; he sent the bones back to the President in Washington.

Lewis also learned some basic medical skills. The expedition would spend much of its time in the wilderness, and would need a "doctor." Lewis already had a background in folk medicine, learned from his mother. Now, Dr. Benjamin Rush provided the explorer with the doctor's booklet, *Rules of Health,* and gave him an ample supply of his own Dr. Rush's Pills for "costiveness," or constipation. The pills were used interchangeably on the trip—for constipation, diarrhea, and countless other ailments. Lewis's methods met with considerable success.

Eventually, Lewis became the principal botanist, naturalist, and doctor on the expedition, while Clark specialized in geography and mapmaking. Both men were curious about the Native American tribes, their customs, and their languages.

President Jefferson gave Lewis and Clark a long list of instructions; the scientists provided supplemental details. The instructions covered almost everything that might arise on the trip. They specified what type of covers the journals (containing the records of the trip) should have: Jefferson wanted the explorers to make copies, some on birch paper, with one copy encased in elk skin to prevent water damage. The President knew these records might be the most important result of the journey.

The expedition left St. Louis on May 13, 1804. The group traveled first by keel boat, then by pirogue, a type of boat made by fastening canoes together with planks. Eventually, as the Missouri River narrowed toward its headwaters, the men used canoes.

Lewis and Clark knew nothing of how long they would be gone, nor of how wide the continent was at that latitude, nor of how difficult the traveling might be. They had learned that the Missouri River originated somewhere in the Rocky Mountains, a range that some Native American tribes called the "Great Shining Mountains." How high or wide the range was, no one could say. Somewhere beyond the mountains the great Columbia River flowed; American ships had visited the Columbia in the past. With luck, the explorers hoped they could travel up the Missouri, make a short portage, and take the Columbia west to the Pacific.

Travel was easy at first, though there were some discipline problems. A man was punished for being drunk on duty—he received 100 lashes. Another was caught sleeping at his post—he was also given 100 lashes. In August, a man deserted. But thereafter the explorers remained close friends (one man did get 75 lashes for "mutinous expression").

More than once Lewis was called on to practice his limited

LEWIS AND CLARK'S WESTWARD JOURNEY, 1804–1805

medical skills. In July, a man suffered from sunstroke. Captain Lewis bled him—a common technique in those days—and the stricken man soon recovered. Another man developed what was described as a "tumor." Lewis drained a pint of fluid from the cyst and the man soon felt better.

One man didn't recover. On August 20, Sergeant Charles Floyd died after an illness of several days. He apparently suffered an attack of appendicitis; he would probably have died even in a good hospital, given the state of medical knowledge in 1804. Floyd's death touched the men deeply. They etched his name, his rank, and the date into a cedar post, and Meriwether Lewis read over his grave. Sargeant Floyd's father had served in the military with William Clark's older brother, and now Clark wrote a touching tribute in his journal:

"This Man at all times gave us proofs of his firmness and Determined resolution to doe Service to his Countrey and honor to himself."

Sargeant Floyd was buried atop a bluff named after him, next to Floyds River. He was the expedition's only fatality.

Another near-tragedy occurred just one week into the trip when Meriwether Lewis lost his footing and fell off a three-hundred-foot-tall cliff. About twenty feet from the top, though, he managed to grab onto a small sapling sprouting from the side of the cliff. Lewis yelled for help, and his companions were able to rescue him.

Every member of the party suffered scrapes, bumps, and bruises, regular colds and intestinal problems. And Lewis was poisoned the day he took his rock collecting too seriously. He applied his own home remedy and was well enough the next day to go look at a buffalo that one of the men had shot—the first buffalo the expedition had seen.

Too soon, winter approached, and the Great Shining Mountains were not yet in sight. Lewis and Clark decided to spend the cold months with the Mandan Indians in what is now North Dakota. With one exception, the tribes along the river had been friendly. Carrying out President Jefferson's instructions, Lewis and Clark had met with leaders of each tribe, presented them with gifts, and informed them that they were now subjects of the American President—the Great White Chief—in the East. The tribes had welcomed the party; the existence of some faraway chief probably meant little to them.

A meeting with the Sioux precipitated the one incident: weapons were drawn on both sides, but the hostility was quickly diffused. The Sioux dominated the Great Plains, yet they, too, were able to coexist with Lewis and Clark.

Winter at Fort Mandan, as the explorers called it, was brutally cold, though not unusually so for the Dakotas. Many of the men suffered frostbite. Lewis was forced to amputate the toes of an Indian boy who had spent a night outdoors during a hunting trip. At Fort Mandan, the party was joined by a French-Canadian trapper named Toussaint Charbonneau and his pregnant wife, Sacagawea.

Sacagawea was a Shoshone Indian. She had been captured as a young girl by a Hidatsa hunting party; the Hidatsa were closely related to the Mandans. Later, Sacagawea was sold to Charbonneau, who took her for his wife. Charbonneau offered their services to the expedition as interpreters, guides, and cooks, and Lewis and Clark quickly hired them.

Charbonneau's only real talent was cooking, though he also knew some of the Indian languages. Other than that, he complained constantly and was of no help in a crisis. Sacagawea, however, turned out to be a valuable addition. Though she could rarely serve as a guide (she was too young when she was taken from her home to the west to remember much), her presence in the party signified to tribes along the way that the explorers' intentions were peaceful: women did not accompany war parties. Many of the tribes might otherwise have been hostile. Thanks in part to Sacagawea, the expedition generally had excellent relations with Native Americans.

Also, Sacagawea was cool in a crisis. In May of 1805, when one of the pirogues capsized, Sacagawea managed to save many valuable supplies while her husband madly swam ashore, in a panic to save himself.

While the party was still at Fort Mandan, Meriwether Lewis was called on to help the young Shoshone woman. She went into labor and her labor was a difficult one. Lewis used an old Indian remedy for Sacagawea's pains. He ground up two rattlesnake rattles and fed the powder to her. To Lewis's surprise, it actually worked—at least Sacagawea gave birth to a healthy boy shortly after the treatment.

In the spring, Lewis sent some of the men back downstream to deliver a collection of scientific samples and Indian artifacts to the President. Lewis included several live animals: four magpies, a prairie dog, and a split-tail grouse. The men left the shipment in St. Louis, and it eventually made its way to New Orleans. After sitting around on the docks for a while, the crates were loaded onto a ship bound for the East Coast. Imagine the surprise of Thomas Jefferson's servant when he opened the crates that were delivered weeks later: there, staring back at him, was the prairie dog and one of the magpies, still alive after all those months of travelling.

After making his shipment, Lewis led the expedition on up the Missouri River. The explorers had some indication of what might be immediately ahead of them: forks in the river, rapids, other tribes. They had asked everyone they met on the way up the Missouri and at the Mandan villages to draw maps of the wilderness ahead, however vague.

Also on their journey from St. Louis, Lewis and Clark had heard stories about the huge grizzly bears of the West. "The men as well as ourselves are anxious to meet some of these bear," Lewis wrote in his journal. Shortly after leaving the Mandan villages, he killed a small grizzly bear. He was unimpressed. Why, he wondered, should such a creature inspire fear? Later, though, he encountered a full-grown grizzly, and his opinion changed immediately to one of respect.

The Great Falls of the Missouri in what is now Montana also earned their respect. Tribes far downriver knew of this huge cataract. Even the Indians' extravagant praise of the natural wonder could not have prepared Lewis and Clark for what they saw. Lewis, usually at ease writing flowery descriptions, could hardly convey his impressions: "I beheld those cataracts with astonishment." Clark was also impressed: "This is one of the grandest views in nature, and by far exceeds anything I ever saw."

The difficulty of the portage around the Great Falls nearly overshadowed their beauty. Lewis and Clark began to doubt whether the Missouri could ever be a Northwest Passage to the Pacific Ocean.

Spirits revived at the sight of the Great Shining Mountains not far beyond the falls and again when Sacagawea began to recognize a few landmarks. The party began their ascent, and traveling became slow and difficult in the mountains. The expedition entered the Bitterroot Mountains—the land of the Shoshones, Sacagawea's people. Sacagawea suspected she was near her native village.

One day, the explorers spotted a Shoshone horseman and called to him. Terrified, he disappeared, and Lewis and a small party set off after him, desperate to find the Shoshone. When they finally located the Shoshone and brought some of them back to Clark, Sacagawea, and the rest of the expedition, in one of western history's amazing coincidences, Sacagawea recognized her long-lost brother. After the years of forced separation, her reunion with her people was a happy one.

The friendly Shoshones helped the white men trade for the horses they sorely needed now that they were traveling on foot. Charbonneau and Sacagawea, though tempted to remain with Sacagawea's people, decided to continue with the expedition.

The group left the Shoshones and crossed the western slopes of the Rockies, traveling through what is now Idaho. The terrain got rougher as they went. Horses stumbled many times, often sending their riders sprawling to the ground. Every man on the expedition suffered cuts and bruises. To make matters worse, there was little to eat. Thus far on the trip, the men had managed to shoot deer, bison, and elk, and to catch fish to eat. But here game was scarce.

It was only fall, but the travelers on horseback found themselves lost in a snowstorm. They might have all died, their journey erased from history, had the Nez Percé not come to their rescue. As they headed out of the Bitterroot Montains, the explorers stumbled upon the Nez Percé who then filled the party's stomachs with food. The expedition members never forgot that kindness.

After bidding the Nez Percé goodbye, the party came upon the Snake River. The explorers once again took to canoes, and despite huge rapids, paddled downstream until they were swirled into the Columbia River itself. Here, to Lewis and Clark's amazement, river tribes had stretched huge fishing weirs across narrow portions of the river, trapping Pacific salmon in their upstream migration. Below waterfalls and rapids, the Indians speared or netted the fish where they congregated to rest.

The party welcomed the addition of salmon to their diet— although these were the unfamiliar Pacific salmon. Though not the first to describe species of Pacific salmon, Lewis and Clark first recorded finding them so far inland. The expedition members quickly discovered an important difference between the western fish and the

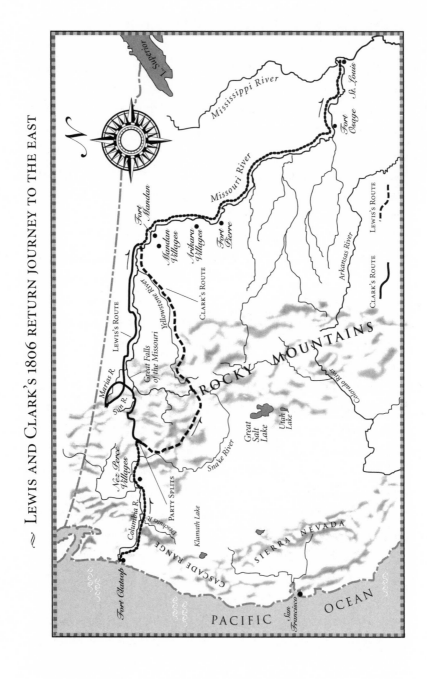

LEWIS AND CLARK'S 1806 RETURN JOURNEY TO THE EAST

more familiar Atlantic salmon of New England: Pacific salmon die after spawning.

As the group pressed on down the Columbia, the great river grew wider each day. On November 7, 1805, the explorers heard a long-awaited sound: the waves of the Pacific Ocean crashing ashore on a western beach. Lewis and Clark stepped into the salty water near present-day Long Beach, Washington, just north of the mouth of the Columbia.

A year and a half after leaving St. Louis, the expedition had reached its goal.

The men delightedly explored north and south from the river mouth, observing sea otters, sea lions, and even a sturgeon. Clark shot an unusual-looking bird—a condor—and drew a picture of it in his journal. He called it a "buzzard of the large size."

As winter was approaching, the party crossed the mile-wide mouth of the Columbia and built winter quarters at Fort Clatsop, in the northwest corner of what is now Oregon.

The winter of 1805–1806 was milder for the explorers than the previous one at Fort Mandan. Along the Pacific Coast there was no snow, but the long periods of rainy weather plagued the party. From November 1805 until the following spring, they counted only twelve days without rain. Clothes were always wet and mildewed and fleas drove the men crazy. The food was monotonous; most of the party had digestive problems.

When the weather permitted, the explorers collected specimens of plants and animals. Clark and Sacagawea and several of the men even went up the coast to inspect a beached whale. They brought back whale blubber for the others to try.

By spring, everyone was anxious to head home. They had hoped to return by ship; Jefferson had given Lewis and Clark letters of credit to book passage home with any ship's captain. There were many signs that American and British ships had visited the mouth of the Columbia. One of the local Clatsop Indian girls even had the name of a sailor, "J. Bowman," tattooed on her arm. But no ships arrived.

The American ship *Lydia* may have visited the Columbia while the expedition was encamped nearby; more likely, the ship arrived a month after the group's departure. Lewis and Clark knew nothing of the *Lydia*, though. They left several documents listing the names of those present at Fort Clatsop, with the local tribe, which eventually handed them over to the *Lydia*'s captain. Much later, sailors delivered the documents to the President.

The return trip to the East took only six months. Lewis and Clark had made careful maps and knew their route. And, the certainty that home was just over the horizon added a quickness to the men's steps and extra strength to their arms paddling their canoes.

Everything did not go smoothly, however. On April 11, along the upper Columbia, Indians stole Lewis's dog, Seaman. Outraged, Lewis sent a party of men armed with guns to rescue the animal. It was the first time either commander had ever ordered "shoot to kill," but Lewis did so and the dog thieves backed down.

The few uneasy moments between the easterners and Indian tribes on the voyage out had ended peacefully. This one did too, when the chief apologized. He blamed "two very bad men" for the incident. The mixing of two cultures may have exacerbated the problem: theft between tribes was more of an accepted custom.

One other encounter on the return trip didn't end so peacefully. It happened after Lewis and Clark decided to take separate routes; each would explore a new part of the Rockies. Since they now had a map, they could plan where to meet again farther east, in order to return together to St. Louis.

While traveling separately, Lewis and three men encountered a group of Blackfeet. The Indians seemed friendly; the explorers had little reason to be wary when they went to sleep on the night of July 26, 1806. At daylight, they were awakened by a shout. Private Joseph fields had carelessly left his rifle unattended and one of the Blackfeet grabbed the weapon, running off with it. Another tried to steal a horse. In the ensuing fight, one Blackfeet was fatally stabbed and Lewis shot and killed another man.

The incident greatly disturbed Lewis. Throughout their journey, relations with Native Americans had been excellent. For decades to come, Blackfeet were bitter toward American settlers and trappers. Any white visitors entering Blackfeet country put themselves in immediate danger.

Lewis also endured his second near-tragedy during this section of the return journey. He and one of his party, a one-eyed woodsman named Peter Cruzatte, had gone out hunting. The two men separated to try their luck. Cruzatte thought he saw a deer creeping through the undergrowth and fired. A man cried out in pain; it was Lewis. Clothed in his buckskin clothes, hidden by thick vegetation, Lewis had resembled a deer. Still, Cruzatte had violated a cardinal rule of hunting: he had fired before positively identifying his target.

The bullet hit Lewis in the upper thigh and rear end, but it passed through the flesh cleanly. He was in pain and couldn't walk or even sit down. Cruzatte, very apologetic, insisted that he truly had been shooting at a deer. Lewis knew better, but he never bore the man ill will; as close travelling companions for more than two years, they had been through too much together. Nevertheless, Lewis was fortunate to be alive, and for several weeks he had to lie on his side in a canoe as the party paddled down the Missouri River.

In mid-August 1806, an excited shout arose from the lead canoe in Lewis's group. They had spotted the unmistakable sliver of smoke from a campfire downstream. It was Clark and the rest of the expedition.

Clark was very concerned about his friend's wounds. He wrote in his journal on August 12: "I examined the wound and found it a very bad flesh wound.... I washed Capt. L wound which has become Sore and Somewhat painfull to him." By September 1, however, Lewis was up and around. A week later, he was almost fully recovered. Relieved, Clark wrote, "My worthy friend, Cap. Lewis has entirely recovered. His wounds are heeled up and he can walk and even run nearly as well as ever he could."

On August 17 at the Mandan villages, Lewis and Clark settled up with Charbonneau and Sacagawea for their long service: $500.33 (and 1/3 of a cent) and two canoes. As the party made progress down the Missouri River, the country looked more and more familiar. They passed several landmarks and the days went quickly. Soon after turning south, they began to encounter small groups of men heading up the Missouri, lured by stories of valleys filled with beaver.

On August 29, Clark walked to the top of a hill and scanned the surrounding plains. He saw vast herds of buffalo (20,000 head, he estimated) and deer. The land was alive and healthy. Clark, though never as reflective in his writing as Lewis, realized the importance of the moment. Once the men reached St. Louis and reported their discoveries to the young nation, many others would follow in their footsteps. Someday, it would not be possible to see such a panorama, to witness such great herds of animals. Both Lewis and Clark sensed that their return would cause a turning point in history.

On September 20, 1806, the expedition passed the small French settlement of La Charette and the men waved to the first white settlers they had seen in more than two years. The men fired their rifles into the air and bought two gallons of whiskey to celebrate.

Soon, they landed in St. Louis. The news quickly spread across the country. Boston's *Columbia Centinel* reported that "A letter from St. Louis (upper Louisiana) dated September 23, 1806, announces the arrival of Captains Lewis and Clark from their expedition to the interior....they have kept an ample journal of their tour, which will be published, and must afford much intelligence."

In two and a half years, Lewis and Clark had covered 7,689 miles. When they arrived in St. Louis, most people were amazed: they had long ago given up the explorers for dead. The two became national heroes. Their men were awarded tracts of land for their service and the two leaders were named to new positions: Lewis was appointed Governor of the Louisiana Territory and Clark became the territory's principal Indian agent, with the rank of brigadier general.

Meriwether Lewis never adapted to his post-expedition life. He was a complex man. On one of his birthdays during the expedition, he wrote in his journal that he hadn't accomplished much in his life. After he returned to St. Louis he became more melancholy. It seems he was unsuited to being an administrator, and his fame made him uneasy. He took to drinking. In September 1809, at a tavern in Natchez Trace, he ended his own life with a pistol.

William Clark, always the more easy going of the two, spent most of the remainder of his career dealing with Indian tribes of the West. He lost a bid to become Governor of Missouri, but served as Superintendent of Indian Affairs out of St. Louis. He died on September 1, 1838, at the age of sixty-nine, at the home of his son, Meriwether Lewis Clark.

The publication of Lewis and Clark's journals was a convoluted process. The unabridged, unedited versions didn't appear before the early twentieth century. Until that time, most people had no concept of the rich storehouse of information the expedition brought back.

When the complete records were eventually published, it became clear that Lewis and Clark had accomplished an amazing number of things. They discovered a route west and mapped the obstacles along the way. They drew extensive maps of the new territory, revealing the width of the continent. Lewis and Clark discovered 200 new species of plants, many of them edible or useful as medicines; and they found 122 new species and subspecies of animals, including the cutthroat trout, the grayling, the pronghorn antelope, and the bighorn sheep. They brought back fascinating journals filled with notes about Native American customs and the languages of the more than fifty tribes they encountered.

Perhaps most importantly, Lewis and Clark opened the door for future explorers to travel to the new lands of the West. ■

~ *Mountain Man*

John Colter

On a hot, humid summer day in 1926, a steam shovel began excavating a field near New Haven, Missouri. These were modern times by any account, and Missouri was a far cry from the wild, western land it had been a hundred years before. The steam-shovel operator surely had no thoughts of those frontier days when his bucket brought forth another load of soil. But the shovel's contents surprised him: the dirt contained human bones. The remains of a human skeleton, long ago covered over by soil and undergrowth, were scattered throughout the bucket load of earth.

The steam-shovel operator stopped his machine and climbed down to study the bones. Who had this unfortunate soul been, and how long had he been buried there? Continuing to pick through the pile, the man found a leather pouch. Its rotting thong was still looped around a portion of the skeleton's vertebrae. The shovel operator gently brushed away decades of dirt and read the name branded on the leather: "Colter."

The operator recognized it. John Colter, perhaps one of the most famous mountain men, was still remembered in parts of Missouri and many areas of the Rocky Mountains. He had been a member of the Lewis and Clark expedition to the Pacific Ocean. Later, he became a trapper in the Rockies. During that time, he stumbled across the incredible sights of Yellowstone—the first white person to see them—and he pulled off one of the most famous escapes from Indian captivity.

A legend in his own lifetime, John Colter was truly a man with sand.

~ ~ ~

John Colter was born in Virginia in 1774 and grew to be a lanky six-footer. In his youth he ventured westward, fought Indians in the Alleghenies, and ended up in Kentucky.

In Kentucky, Colter happened upon an opportunity of a lifetime. William Clark was recruiting experienced frontiersmen for a grand expedition into the unexplored lands of western North America. He needed men who could hunt, live under difficult conditions, and act with confidence in the wild. John Colter convinced Clark of his merits. Before Meriwether Lewis arrived from the East, Colter had signed up to join the Corps of Discovery as one of the "nine Kentuckians."

Private Colter became a valuable member of the Lewis and Clark Expedition. He never received a promotion during the two-and-a-half-year expedition, but he was extremely reliable and resourceful. Lewis and Clark gave the thirty-year-old many important responsibilities and assignments.

The lengthy journey to the Pacific and back was difficult and dangerous. Long before the expedition returned safely, most people in the East assumed the explorers had all died.

Those who made the journey had experience that the developing American fur trade found attractive: the men were among the very

Fur Trappers

few to have traveled the width of the Rocky Mountains. They knew the country, the distances, and the richest areas for beaver. They also knew many of the native tribes, as well as some of their languages and customs.

John Colter had marketable skills, and he took advantage of them. Shortly before reaching the Mandan villages on the way back to St. Louis, the Lewis & Clark Expedition met up with Joseph Dixon and Forrest Hancock. Dixon and Hancock planned to trap in the virgin lands themselves, becoming the first true mountain men. These easterners had some trapping experience, but for the most part they looked on the wild lands of the upper Missouri as a great adventure. They invited John Colter to be their guide and partner.

Colter asked for an early discharge; Lewis and Clark agreed, on the condition that no other member of the party be allowed to make such a request. Colter had been a loyal soldier during the long journey. The leaders expected to be back in St. Louis within a month, so they bid Colter farewell and continued downstream.

Colter and his partners traveled upstream by canoe. Eventually, they set up camp in the Yellowstone Valley, trapping during the winter of 1806–1807. The bitter cold and deep snows of winter in the Rockies were too much for Dixon and Hancock. In the spring, the two men parted ways with Colter and returned to St. Louis and civilization.

Colter thought about returning to the East too. He had been away for three years. By summer, he was lonesome for home. Alone, his canoe piled with pelts, Colter headed back down the Missouri River, intending to go as far as St. Louis.

Fate intervened again, this time in the form of a persuasive entrepreneur named Manuel Lisa. Lisa had formed the Missouri Fur Company and intended to dominate the American fur trade on the

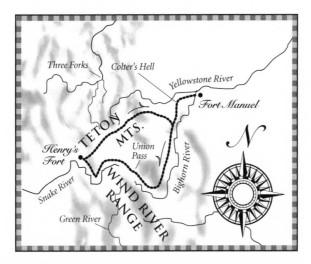

~ Colter's Exploration of 1807–1808, a scouting and
trapping trip authorized by Manuel Lisa.

upper Missouri River. He had recruited forty-two trappers—including several former members of the Lewis and Clark Expedition—and headed west.

The party traveled light, carrying only enough food to last until they reached the Platte River. The upriver area was rich in game, and they planned to live off the land.

They had barely enough: by the time the party set up camp at the Platte in July 1807, stores were down to a quarter pound of meat per man per day. They had miscalculated: this was Sioux country, where game was uncommonly scarce.

Then they saw a lone man paddling a canoe full of pelts downstream: John Colter. Colter would have been excited to see anyone, and here he found several friends. Manuel Lisa must have added persuasion to the camaraderie; instead of returning to the East as he had planned, Colter joined the Lisa party as a guide and trapper. He lived in the wild country of the Rockies for another three and a half years, a short time which turned out to contain a lifetime of adventures.

The life of a fur trapper was never easy. But these men—some on their own, some employed by others—traveled the wild country in close harmony with the land. Before steel traps became common in the late 1820s, trappers like Colter used the Indian method of catching a beaver. They snared it, then clubbed or shot the animal to kill it. In later years, trappers had to carry five or six heavy iron traps around with them.

The mountain men wore clothes of buckskin or wool, with leather leggings for traveling through the undergrowth. They often wore moccasins made of buffalo or deerskin. Their own skin was brown from months or years in the sun. Sometimes trappers worked alone, but often they traveled in pairs or threes, looking for beaver sign in slow-moving waters, trapping what they could, then moving on.

If beaver were sparse, the trappers might become traders. The Crow were especially good trading partners. Crow women knew how to preserve pelts. They had learned the technique from Antoine Larocque, a French trapper with the British Northwest Company. If Manuel Lisa's trappers couldn't come up with sufficient furs on their own, Lisa traded for pelts with the Crow.

By late 1807, Manuel Lisa's dream of dominating the American fur trade had not come true. Taking a new tack, he set out to entice Native American tribes to come to his fort at the confluence of the Yellowstone and Bighorn rivers; there they could trade furs for trinkets and store goods. Lisa entrusted John Colter with the task of tracking down the tribes and inviting them to his fort. Few other individuals, even if they had known the territory, had the stamina and perseverance to do the job.

As winter approached, Colter plunged alone into the wilderness, carrying (as usual) just the bare essentials: a buckskin shirt and leggings over pants, a buckskin jacket, a buffalo robe for sleeping, a thirty-pound pack containing salt, tobacco, and a few supplies, trinkets for trade with the tribes, a rifle, and ammunition.

Colter's mission was to issue as many invitations to Lisa's fort as possible. He began by skirting the eastern flank of the Absaroka Range. He came upon a Crow camp at the upper end of the Wind River Valley. From there, during the winter of 1807–1808, he made a grueling trek across the Wind River Range. At Union Gap, he crossed the Continental Divide, crisscrossed the Snake River several times, and turned eastward toward what is now called Jackson Hole, and the Grand Tetons.

Though he was accustomed to seeing the grandeur of nature, John Colter found the Tetons spectacular. Their jagged, snow-covered spires jutted into the sky. Colter was the first white man to gaze on this region (which today covers part of Idaho, Wyoming, and Montana). And the wondrous sights were only beginning.

Traveling eastward, in the distance Colter saw what appeared to be dozens of campfires sending smoke into the sky. He approached with care and encountered such sights as had never been seen before by the civilized world. There were geysers shooting sprays of water and steam hundreds of feet in the air; there were pools of bubbling mud and boiling hot springs. Colter must have feared he had entered the bowels of hell. In the distance, he saw the enormous lake now known as Yellowstone.

The Yellowstone region is riddled with thermal pockets, many of them quite large. Colter never saw some of the more spectacular sites, but those along the Shoshone River—known for a time as the Stinking River or Stinkingwater—were bizarre enough. When he eventually returned to Lisa's fort, he couldn't stop talking about what he had seen. No one believed him.

Even years later, when he told genteel citizens of St. Louis about boiling mud and rocks that sprayed water, no one believed a word. The seemingly mythical place he described became known among fur trappers as "Colter's Hell." Later, Washington Irving popularized the nickname in his writing.

John Colter's travels with Lewis and Clark had secured him a place in western history. His five-hundred-mile journey through the Rocky Mountains, alone and in winter, and his description of the wonders he saw, added to his renown. But his most famous adventure was still to come.

In the fall of 1808, Colter and another veteran trapper, John Potts, were trapping in Blackfeet country. Both men felt uneasy, especially John Colter. Ever since Meriwether Lewis and his men killed two Blackfeet braves during an incident in 1806, tensions had remained high between the Blackfeet and white intruders.

John Colter had not been with Lewis at the time, but in the spring of 1808, Colter had had his own incident with the Blackfeet. While he was staying at a Crow camp, inviting them to trade furs with Lisa, the Crow were attacked by a party of Blackfeet. Colter was forced to join his hosts in repelling the aggressors. During the battle, Colter killed at least one Blackfeet Indian. White men were an unusual sight, and John Colter became a marked man.

So, when Colter and Potts beached their canoe in Blackfeet country in the fall of 1808, and they were quickly surrounded by a large band of Blackfeet, they froze. Colter knew escape was futile. Potts, however, reached for his rifle. His body was quickly riddled with arrows. The Blackfeet grabbed Colter, took his furs, rifle, and trappings, and led him back to their village.

In most instances, the Blackfeet tortured their prisoners— whether white or Indian. The enemy endured a slow, painful death.

For some time, his captors argued about how Colter would die. The tribal elders were particularly anxious to torture Colter since he had killed Blackfeet in the past.

This time, the Blackfeet decided to give their prisoner a sporting chance, though not much of one. They stripped Colter to the skin and motioned for him to start running. Clearly, the warriors were going to hunt him down for sport.

Colter started off slowly while the Blackfeet taunted and hooted at him. Finally, when he had reached the end of a long meadow and was some four hundred yards away, dozens of the younger braves took off after him. The race was on—a race for John Colter's life.

What the Blackfeet didn't know was that Colter was an extremely fast runner. When he heard them start after him, he began to run for real. He was shoeless, unclothed, and unarmed, but he just kept running.

Like most competent outdoorsmen, John Colter had a good sense of direction. So, even though he was running in a panic, Colter knew where he was headed. If he could reach the Madison River, he told himself, he might have a chance. But the river was six miles away and already he felt the wind of arrows and lances as they flew past his naked body. Colter's feet were cracked and bleeding from the rough ground and his legs were punctured by the thorns of prickly pear, but he kept running.

Most people would have collapsed from exhaustion. But John Colter was no ordinary man. Mile after mile, he drove himself onward, until blood streamed from his nose and mouth. He looked back and saw that most of the Blackfeet were lagging some distance behind. The prey had more stamina than the predators. Only one warrior—clearly the best runner of the village—kept pace. And he was gaining on his bleeding victim.

As Colter stumbled around a cluster of trees, he saw his chance. He crouched suddenly, waited in ambush, then tripped his pursuer and wrestled him to the ground. With strength gained by a high level of adrenaline, Colter grabbed his attacker's lance and plunged the blade into the man's chest.

In an instant, Colter had regained his feet and started running again. Looking back, he saw the other warriors pause over the body of their fallen companion. This gave him the edge he needed. The gap widened and John Colter kept running.

Panting and heaving, Colter rounded a bluff and caught sight of the deep, fast-moving river. Without a second's hesitation, he dove in and let the current carry him some distance downstream. Eventually, he came to a logjam of debris that the river had deposited during previous high water.

Colter hid under the driftwood for hours, thankful that the moving water drowned out the sound of his heavy breathing. He watched the Blackfeet search the banks for signs of his passing. Since he had come downstream by water, he had left no tracks. It was autumn and the water temperature was cooling rapidly, but Colter stayed hidden until dark. By then the Blackfeet had given up. Finally, he emerged from beneath the logjam and swam downstream for another several miles.

When Colter did finally leave the water, he started running again. The odds were still against him—he was naked, unarmed, and far from home. Rankled at losing their prey, the Blackfeet would be back again at daybreak. So, John Colter just kept running. For seven days and more than one hundred and fifty miles, he ran, walked, and crawled until he finally reached Lisa's fort.

The emaciated man who emerged from the woods must have been a sight. His feet were shredded and coated with blood, his legs were festering with wounds from the thorns, and his naked body was gaunt from starvation and exhaustion. His close friends didn't recognize him until he said his name.

John Colter had accomplished one of the greatest feats of survival in western lore, and had made it back to safety. His story was retold for decades. Within only a few weeks, Colter was newly outfitted and back in the mountains.

Colter tempted fate once more in early 1810, again at the hands of the Blackfeet. He was traveling with a party of trappers when a band of Blackfeet warriors surprised them. A vicious battle ensued. As Colter fired at the Blackfeet, five of his companions were killed around him.

John Colter realized that he was living on borrowed time. He asked God for help. "If God will only forgive me this time, and let me off," he later recalled having prayed, "I will leave this country day after tomorrow—and be damned if I ever come into it again."

Colter's prayers were answered. He managed to slip away into the darkness. Returning to Lisa's fort, he announced to the others that he was as good as his word. He set off in a canoe the next morning and, without a backward glance, paddled two thousand miles downriver to St. Louis.

John Colter never did go back into the mountains. Vowing to live a more genteel life, he married a Missouri woman, Nancy Hooker, and settled on a small farm. But John Colter was no farmer. When he died in November of 1813, penniless, his wife simply left his body in their tiny cabin, his leather pouch upon his chest. She had no money for a coffin or a burial. She headed for Illinois, never to return.

The most famous mountain man of his time, John Colter never kept a journal of his life. Colter's knowledge of the Rocky Mountains helped William Clark prepare the first definitive map of the Northwest. And even in the twentieth century, people remembered hearing his name.

Only when those mysterious bones were unearthed in 1926 was the final chapter written on John Colter. Inside the leather pouch were fur receipts and notebooks—still legible. This time, the local residents made sure that the mountain man's remains were properly buried. ■

⁓ Spanish-American Fur Trader

Manuel Lisa

*T*he journey had not been an easy one for Manuel Lisa. He had invested most of his savings in it and had organized a company of forty-two men himself. Just as the party was setting off, he had to return to town and bail one of his men out of jail. Then, as they poled their keelboats up the Missouri River, their food supplies started to dwindle. Lisa had assumed that wild game would be plentiful, but their hunting forays turned up nothing edible. The men were down to strict rations

The expedition had had the good fortune not to encounter any Sioux while traveling through Sioux lands. But now they were in Arikara country, and any delay could force the half-starved men to turn back. Just as Lisa was pondering their dilemma, and saying a silent prayer that luck would smile on them, one of the bow men gave an excited shout. Along the bank were several hundred warriors.

The Arikara were one of the most dangerous of the tribes along the Missouri. Many men who had underestimated them—white and Indian alike—paid for the mistake with their lives. The Arikara warriors, or "Rees," as the traders called them, were unpredictable.

Lisa had his own philosophy of how to deal with the Indians. But before he could act on it, the Arikara were firing arrows at the two keelboats. The explorers ducked and grabbed their rifles. Quickly, Lisa ordered his men to drop their weapons and land the boats amongst the shouting warriors. This seemed to defuse the tensions.

Soon, the Arikara women stepped forward with items for trade. But one warrior started shouting at the strangers and slashing their bags of grain with his lance. Lisa now commanded his men to draw their weapons and point the boat-mounted guns toward the aggressor.

Perhaps because the Arikara were startled, perhaps because Manuel Lisa had an unusual sense of how to deal with people, the threat worked. The Arikara brought forth pipes. Lisa smoked with the chiefs and gave them numerous gifts, and the boats were allowed to pass upriver without further incident.

The Arikara had taught Lisa something: the Plains tribes respected strength and bravery. These Indians expected others to speak the truth and to keep their word. These were valuable lessons that helped Manuel Lisa develop relations of mutual respect with most Native Americans.

Many other people did not like Manuel Lisa; few were neutral on the subject. People either despised him or grudgingly respected his business abilities. More than once, Lisa fought an employee with his fists. He learned never to turn his back on anyone—even his own men. Some described him as ruthless and unscrupulous. One employee said that "rascality sat on every aspect of his dark-complexioned Mexican face." (The employee was mistaken: Lisa was not Mexican.)

When Manuel Lisa and his partner, Francois Benoit, outfitted the Lewis and Clark Expedition, Meriwether Lewis found the result so unsatisfactory that he wrote to William Clark, "Damn Manuel and triply damn Mr. B. They gave me more vexation and trouble than their lives are worth."

Yet Manuel Lisa was unquestionably one of the most important figures in the American fur trade of the early nineteenth century. On many occasions, he traveled into the wilds himself. More often, he hired and organized others to travel throughout the Rocky Mountains. In their search for beaver and other furs, these men extended white civilization and discovered new lands. Despite his complex reputation, Lisa managed to play a very important role in the exploration of the American West.

Manuel Lisa's parents were Spanish. He may have been born in Cuba or Louisiana; he grew up in New Orleans. Young Lisa learned to speak several languages and soon moved easily among the French traders of Louisiana and St. Louis.

Lisa was a smart businessman from the start. Quick to spot an opportunity, he dealt in land, slaves, goods, furs—anything that might make a profit. Rumors circulated that he gained government contracts through bribes. With Manuel Lisa, anything was possible. Many of his schemes lost him money. In 1797, he bought 2,000 acres of land in Indiana for $1,700; he hardly ever visited it because he was too busy dealing in other commodities.

In 1798, Lisa arrived in St. Louis. He immediately saw opportunities for trading with the Indian tribes along the lower Missouri River. In the era before the Louisiana Purchase, the government awarded exclusive trading rights for areas in the West. The rights Lisa wanted were owned by a small group of French businessmen. Lisa took them on—especially the powerful Chouteau brothers—petitioning for an end to monopolies. In a free market, Lisa knew, he would be able to out-compete anyone.

Lisa became a marked man in the local business community. He was even thrown in jail for a while. That didn't deter him; the man thrived on adversity. When the United States acquired the Louisiana Territory, the practice of exclusive rights ended and Manuel Lisa got his foot in the door.

Lisa first followed opportunity to the Southwest. The governments of New Spain and the United States had both barred trade between the United States and Santa Fe. Because of the embargo, goods had to be brought to Santa Fe from Mexico. Explorer Zebulon Pike later gave accounts of the Santa Fe region's resources: it provided its residents with sheep, venison, tobacco, furs, buffalo robes, salt, and "[w]rought copper vessels of a superior quality." Everything else had to be imported—at a high cost.

Long before Pike arrived in the area, Manuel Lisa had the situation figured out. He intended to make a tidy profit on goods brought from St. Louis. There was still that pesky ban on trade—but maybe he could find a loophole in the law.

Lisa teamed up with an elderly trader named Jacques Clamorgan and got Clamorgan to apply for a license to trade with the Pawnee tribe. The two planned to transport trade goods to a Pawnee camp located near Santa Fe, establish friendly relations with the tribe, and entice residents of Santa Fe to make the short trip to buy their discounted goods. Lisa and Clamorgan believed that if trouble arose with Spanish soldiers, the Pawnees would protect them.

The scheme could have proved lucrative, but Lisa ran into bad luck: James Wilkinson, the acting governor of the Louisiana Territory, found out about the plan. Wilkinson ordered Zebulon Pike, who

MANUEL LISA

Missouri Historical Society, St. Louis

had just embarked on his military/exploring expedition across the Southwest, to "take all prudent and lawful means" to stop Lisa. It later turned out that Wilkinson himself hoped to establish a trading operation to Santa Fe, and he didn't want competition. In his letter to Pike, he referred to Manuel Lisa as a "black Spaniard."

To avoid trouble, Lisa publicly disavowed his plan. Then he had Clamorgan secretly start the trading operation. In August 1807, Clamorgan left St. Louis with four other men and four pack mules loaded with trade goods. He arrived in the Santa Fe region four months later and eventually sold his goods in Chihuahua. Clamorgan was the first man to make a trading journey from the United States to Santa Fe and return with profits—a large part of which went to Manuel Lisa.

Lisa made one other attempt to establish a Santa Fe trade route, but his agent, Charles Sanguinet, lost all his goods in an Indian attack. All things considered, continuing with southwestern trade seemed too risky. Even before Clamorgan returned from his trip, Manuel Lisa set his sights on something more lucrative: the Missouri River fur trade.

Lewis and Clark had just returned to St. Louis from the lands of the western Louisiana Purchase. They brought word of Rocky Mountain valleys teeming with beaver and other animals. Any gentleman worth his salt required at least one beaver hat; the demand for pelts was rising. Lisa figured that St. Louis was ideally located to be the conduit for the furs. Once in St. Louis, they could be sent south to New Orleans and across to Europe, or by river and wagon to the East.

Only one link was missing: someone who could get the furs from the mountains down the river to St. Louis. Manuel Lisa jumped into the gap. He persuaded two investors, Pierre Menard and William Morrison of Illinois, to finance his effort to monopolize the fur trade.

And in April 1807, Lisa launched the first large commercial expedition to the West.

Lisa filled his two keelboats with an estimated $16,000 in trade goods and forty-two hunters and trappers. Several former members of the Lewis and Clark expedition signed on with Lisa; their experience in the upper Missouri made them valuable assets. Unfortunately, not all Lisa's men turned out to be so reliable. Soon after the boats set off, Lisa had to return to St. Louis to bail out John Baptiste Bouché.

As in any such enterprise as this, according to the custom of the time, Bouché had signed a contract that bound him to his employer for a set period. Also as usual, Lisa had advanced Bouché and the others a portion of their wages to settle debts and buy personal supplies for the upcoming months or even years.

Local merchants were often more than willing to offer credit to men who had signed on an expedition. If a man drank too much and ran up a large bill at a tavern, his employer would likely pay the debt, since he already had money invested in the person. Bouché took advantage of the arrangement. Having spent his advance and then some, he landed in jail. Before the local authorities would allow him to journey upriver, Lisa had to pay the man's debts.

Unfortunately for Lisa, Bouché had already spent the larger part of his entire salary. As a result, he refused to do much work. He caused delays by his repeated absences and was accused of stealing food at a time when rations had to be cut to only a quarter pound of meat per day.

This occurred at the mouth of the Platte River, where the expedition set up camp in the vain hope of finding wild game to eat. Here, Lisa's men encountered John Colter, paddling a canoe full of pelts downriver after more than three years in the wilderness. Colter, a veteran of the Lewis and Clark expedition, had spent another year in the

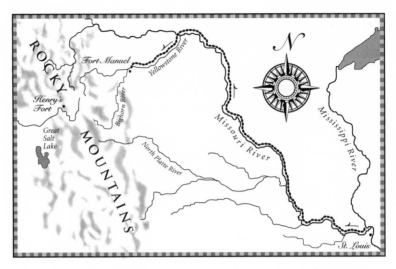

~ Lisa's commercial expedition up the Missouri
River to the Yellowstone River, 1807.

Rockies trapping beaver. He joined the group and proved to be an important addition. Whatever Manuel Lisa's personality faults, he had the reputation of relying on the experience and advice of subordinates.

The party left its camp, traveled through Sioux country, and overcame the hostility of the Arikara. Moving on, they entered the land of the Mandan, who generally had good relations with whites. Lisa walked alone into each Mandan village, demonstrating that he was a man to be respected. He met with tribal elders and presented gifts. In the third village he visited, he encountered some resentment; but, by remaining resolute, he won over those Mandan as well.

Upriver, a potentially volatile incident with the Assiniboins was averted. Hundreds of the Indians confronted the explorers; Lisa later reported that "The whole prairie was red with them." Again, Lisa seemed to know what to do. He ordered his men to fire their weapons, including the more powerful boat guns, into the air. Perhaps surprised, perhaps frightened by this display, the Assiniboins ran off.

These stories attest to Manuel Lisa's ability to deal peacefully with the Plains tribes. Several other groups followed Lisa upriver that year; none were as lucky. Indians killed some travelers and forced others to turn back.

Lisa continued on. John Colter recommended the area between the Big Horn and Yellowstone rivers as a destination. There they could build a fort that would serve as the center of their trading and trapping operations. Lisa named their outpost Fort Raymond after his young son back in St. Louis. Later, more often than not, people called it Fort Manuel.

Because the westward trip to Fort Raymond had taken so long, the party arrived late in the Yellowstone country. Lisa had few pelts to show for his efforts so far. In order to build up his supply of furs, Lisa decided to trade with the Native Americans. He selected John Colter for the job of contacting the Crow and other tribes and inviting them to trade furs at Fort Raymond in the spring.

Colter set off on his long, difficult trek in the winter of 1807–1808. George Drouillard, another Lewis and Clark veteran, also did some traveling, exploring the Tongue and Big Horn basins. In the meantime, Lisa's men hunted game and trapped beavers in local waters. Fortunately, the land was rich in animals.

In the spring, tribes arrived with furs in hand and left with blankets, trinkets, and various trade goods. The white trappers were quite successful as well. They brought animals to a scaffold erected near the fort or pelts directly to Lisa. By summer, it was obvious that Lisa and his investors would make a handsome profit. Manuel and several men hauled their stockpile of furs downstream—and right into jail.

Earlier, one of Lisa's men had deserted, taking his pay advance and a considerable amount of stolen supplies. Lisa was livid. He ordered another trapper, George Drouillard, to bring the thief back "dead or alive." Drouillard succeeded, but the deserter, Antoine Bissonette, had been shot and wounded. He was taken to a doctor for medical attention; he later died. Warrants were issued for Drouillard and Lisa's arrest.

At a well-publicized trial, the men cleared themselves by proving Bissonette was a deserter and "a rascal who got what he deserved." The episode caused only a minor distraction. Manuel Lisa's fur expedition to the wilds of the Rocky Mountains was considered a great success.

Manuel Lisa also had an idea that would require extra money: he wanted to change the set up of his fur operations. Lisa had run into problems obtaining furs from the North American tribes. The Plains Indians were nearer, but were not as accustomed to trapping as were some of the mountain tribes. And no tribe seemed ready to kill as many beaver as the traders wanted.

Lisa envisioned a new system: he would hire his own trappers, thus eliminating the Indians from the trading cycle. By continuing to provide the tribes with gifts, he would ensure their good will and safe passage for his men. Overall, he would have more control of the supply of pelts.

Local businessmen may have despised and envied Lisa, but they knew the Spaniard was on the verge of monopolizing the Missouri River fur trade. They jumped on the bandwagon: Lisa had no lack of investors. For his part, he welcomed more outside money. If this new venture was to succeed, he would need to establish more trading posts along the Missouri and hire more men. This would take considerable funds.

Lisa ushered in the era of the "mountain man," a new breed of western trappers. Some earned a salary; others were dependent on their own skills to catch and sell enough pelts to survive or even prosper. All were adventurers, prepared to live a rugged life.

During the winter of 1808–1809, Manuel Lisa and nine partners formed the St. Louis Missouri Fur Company. William Clark (of Lewis and Clark fame) was elected President of the Board; Reuben Lewis— Meriwether Lewis's brother—was another partner; and the rest were St. Louis businessmen. The company came to be known simply as the Missouri Fur Company. It dominated the fur trade for over a decade.

In June 1809, the company's first big expedition left St. Louis with 172 men, 9 barges, and a canoe. The barges contained enough supplies and trade goods to outfit five or six trading posts. The party distributed gifts to tribes along the Missouri and trapped and traded in the fall of 1809. Andrew Henry was the field captain, the man in charge of the expedition.

Henry's men spent the winter at Fort Raymond. In the spring of 1810, the party moved farther up the Missouri to the Three Forks area in the heart of Blackfeet country. The Blackfeet didn't leave the white men in peace for long. Even trappers who traveled in pairs were set upon by Blackfeet, as were the traders.

Pierre Menard, one of Lisa's partners who had accompanied the expedition, soon had enough of such troubles. He loaded the pelts they had on hand onto a boat, took a few men, and headed back to St. Louis.

Andrew Henry decided to strengthen his defenses and stick it out. Half the men would always stay behind to guard the fort while the others hunted for beaver. His precautions weren't enough against the Blackfeet, though. One party of trappers, acting a little carelessly, managed to get itself attacked just two miles from the fort; three men were killed. Other parties lost guns, furs, and horses.

Henry decided life was too dangerous in Blackfeet country. He abandoned the fort in the summer of 1810 and led the men to safer territory. After crossing the Continental Divide, the party discovered the North Fork of the Snake River (now known as the Henry's Fork) and built a trading post near what is now St. Anthony, Idaho. Henry's post consisted of just a few temporary cabins, but it represented a significant achievement: it was the first American settlement west of the Rocky Mountains.

Life wasn't pleasant at the new post. Winter brought heavy snows and extreme cold. The party had little food. The men killed their horses for meat in order to survive. Trappers seldom ate beaver; when they did, as a last resort, they soaked the meat for several hours before cooking it.

In the spring, the men divided into three groups. One group headed toward the Spanish settlements of the Southwest. In an attempt to link up with Spanish trading posts, these men blazed new routes. Their business attempts were only partly successful; they did manage to contact the Arapahos, who traded regularly with the Spanish.

The second group went east to the Grand Tetons. John Colter had come upon these majestic peaks the winter he was soliciting fur trade from the various tribes. He had spread word of the Tetons' beauty and trapping potential. Both parties kept their eyes peeled for beaver; Lisa's agents offered bounties to those who brought in pelts.

Andrew Henry led the third group back to the fort at Three Forks then down the Missouri. On the river, they ran into Manuel Lisa, who was heading upstream with supplies. Henry delivered forty packs of beaver pelts (worth $10 to $20 thousand) and bid his employer good-bye. He continued on to St. Louis, where he retired from the fur business.

In 1811, Lisa sent another party out. Led by Jean Champlain and Ezekiel Williams, this group was to scour the northern Spanish country, where some of Henry's men had looked for trade routes. The party reached the upper Arkansas River and spent the winter hunting and trapping. Here, too, hostile tribes eventually drove them out.

Some of the men went south to Santa Fe. Williams and the others attempted to return to the East, but Indians spotted them and attacked. Everyone except Williams was killed. The trapper managed to hide his furs and escape, reaching St. Louis in September 1813. The next spring, Williams went back and retrieved his furs.

When the other companies saw Williams's furs, they determined to send trappers to the region. Manuel Lisa felt the prospects were too dangerous. Despite the geographical knowledge of the area Ezekiel Williams had brought back, Lisa again abandoned his dream of a commercial trade route to Santa Fe.

These trapping and exploring adventures were typical of Manuel Lisa's "reign" in the fur business. He was a leader with tremendous drive and determination, and he expected the same from those he employed. His men were a hard lot, but Lisa was harder. He had to deal with desertion and theft, laziness and grumbling from the men.

Edward Rose, a mulatto who had lived with the Osage Indians, and who once got into an argument with Lisa, furnishes a typical example. Following the Indian way, Rose at one point gave away most of his possessions as a gesture of generosity. Some of those items belonged to his employer, Lisa. A shouting match between the two turned into a fist fight; only the efforts of another trapper kept the fight from being worse. Lisa promptly climbed into a canoe and paddled downriver. But Rose wasn't through. He grabbed a rifle and fired several shots at the disappearing canoe. Yet, later, Lisa forgave Rose and hired him back.

Conflicts of personality meant little to Manuel Lisa. He put all his trust in business, and in those who had the knowledge and the fortitude to help him be successful. And he was successful. During his best year—more than a decade before the peak of the fur trade—he made $35 thousand. It was a fortune. And because of his many partnerships, Lisa owned a piece of almost everything that was involved in the St. Louis fur trade. His holdings included a fleet of river boats that carried supplies and furs back and forth between upriver trading posts and the buyers and businessmen in St. Louis.

When hostilities with the English erupted into the War of 1812, the United States Government turned to Manuel Lisa. No one had better relations with the tribes of the Missouri River than he. Posted as a government agent for the Upper Missouri, he was credited with keeping the tribes peaceful during the War despite British attempts to stir them up against the Americans.

Manuel Lisa carried his entrepreneurship into his personal life too. He was married three times: twice to white women and once to an Omaha Indian girl named Mitain. That marriage caused upraised eyebrows in St. Louis, but it cemented Lisa's friendship with the Omaha tribe. Manuel and Mitain had two children and Lisa proved himself a devoted father.

To the surprise of many, Lisa had an appreciation for other activities that lacked a direct monetary reward. He and the renowned botanist, Thomas Nutall, had once met in Pennsylvania, and had become fast friends. In 1811, when Nutall and British botanist John Bradbury were wandering the West on their most important collecting trip, Lisa invited them to accompany one of his expeditions for a while. Another time, Lisa's keelboat carried different notables: Sacagawea, her husband Toussaint Charbonneau, and their son.

The career and life of Manuel Lisa ended on August 12, 1820. He died in his sleep at a health spa at the age of forty-nine. Although the Missouri Fur Company survived him, it did not last long. Without Manuel Lisa's supervision, the most powerful force in the fur trade for the first quarter of the nineteenth century was reduced to local trading around what is now Omaha, Nebraska. The company, too, eventually died.

Manuel Lisa accomplished great things in his life. He set up successful guidelines for commerce in the upper Missouri. He established trading posts that centralized trade. He maintained peaceful relations with Native Americans, as no one had done before. And, he initiated the system of free trappers, those enterprising men who explored much of the Rocky Mountains. The era of the mountain man lasted at least two decades beyond Lisa's death. ■

CHAPTER FIVE

∿ Mission from the General

Zebulon Pike

O ne of the men had reported seeing two riders silhouetted against the hillside. But several days had passed and no one had appeared. The man was still weak from recent hardships, so Zebulon Pike had passed the report off as the hallucination of a sick man.

But what he saw now, coming into the valley, was no illusion. One hundred Spanish soldiers, mounted and resplendent in their uniforms, descended from that same ridge and quickly approached the small stockade the Americans had constructed.

Had Pike tried to resist, his small command would have been greatly outnumbered. Resisting was not his intention. The soldiers surrounded the American explorers and took up their positions. A young Spanish officer asked Pike why he was camped on Spanish land. Zebulon Pike looked perplexed. He pointed to the small stream nearby. "What!" he cried. "Is this not the Red River?"

The officer shook his head. No, he said patiently, this was not the Red River. It was the Conejos River, a tributary to the Rio Grande. The Americans had trespassed far inside New Spain. Since they were soldiers flying an American flag over Spanish lands, they would be considered spies.

No one will ever know just how "lost" Zebulon Pike was when Spanish troops captured him on February 26, 1807. If he was really confused about his whereabouts, it wasn't the first time. Suspicions persist that, lost or not, Pike deliberately let himself wander well into Spanish territory—because he had secret orders.

Zebulon Montgomery Pike was born January 5, 1779, in Lamberton, New Jersey. His family moved to Pennsylvania when he was still a child. At the age of fifteen, Pike began a military career in his father's regiment in Indiana Territory. The elder Pike, also named Zebulon, was a veteran of the Revolutionary War.

Young Zeb served at a series of frontier military posts—Fort Allegheny, Fort Massac, Fort Knox, Fort Washington, and Fort Kaskaskia—and was promoted to ensign in 1799, when he was twenty years old.

He may have been small—a fellow officer once described him as five feet, eight inches tall, sturdy, and robust—but Zeb Pike was a born leader. Usually a quiet person, Pike enforced a strong discipline among his men. He believed that fortitude and determination were essential traits for anyone to have, and he led by example.

Pike also valued education. He had only received very basic formal schooling, but he was a lifelong student. Zeb read everything he could find on military strategy, and he taught himself French, Spanish, and mathematics. He also learned the rudiments of many scientific fields.

On furlough in Cincinnati, Pike surprised everyone by falling in love with and marrying Clarissa Brown, the daughter of General John Brown of Kentucky. The couple had three children, two of whom died young. The third child would eventually marry the son of President William Henry Harrison.

Pike's first major assignment came in 1805, when he was a twenty-six-year-old first lieutenant. General James Wilkinson, then Governor of the Louisiana Territory, took notice of Pike (Wilkinson later became Pike's mentor). The chance preferment would prove at times lucky and at others unfortunate.

General Wilkinson gave Pike orders to lead an expedition up the Mississippi. He was charged with finding the great river's source, inviting Indian chiefs to visit General Wilkinson in St. Louis, and negotiating with Native American tribes to obtain land for future military posts.

Lieutenant Pike and twenty soldiers set out to complete the mission "before the waters [were] frozen up." His journal for the trip began with a straightforward entry: "Sailed from my encampment, near St. Louis, at 4 p.m., on Friday, the 9th of August, 1805, with one sergeant, two corporals, and seventeen privates, in a keel-boat 70 feet long, provisioned for four months."

The company unfurled the boat's sail and made good progress up the Mississippi. Near the mouth of the Des Moines River, Pike met with a group of Sac Indians; he continued upriver on August 21. Near present-day Dubuque, Iowa, the expedition passed some valuable lead mines and had soon left the northernmost fort of the Mississippi Valley at Prairie du Chien behind.

On September 23, Pike encountered a group of Sioux living near the Falls of St. Anthony (now St. Paul, Minnesota). He urged the Sioux to make peace with the Chippewa tribes of the region. He also asked for land at the falls and at the mouth of the St. Croix River; the young

United States intended to expand its frontier forts northward and, eventually, westward.

"They gave me the land required, about 100,000 acres, equal to $200,000," Pike reported. "I gave them presents to the amount of about $200, and as soon as the council was over, I allowed the traders to present them with some liquor, which, with what I myself gave, was equal to 60 gallons."

Pike had just concluded Minnesota's first real-estate deal. For a few hundred dollars worth of trinkets and whiskey, the Army received over 100,000 acres that would one day accommodate the city of St. Paul.

On October 16, the expedition members—now in smaller boats—encountered heavy snows. Near Little Falls they constructed log cabins to serve as their winter base. Before winter arrived in force, they built up a supply of game to supplement the stores they had brought with them.

On December 10, Pike pushed northward with a few men on sleds, leaving most of the party behind at Little Falls. The smaller group mapped their route as they went. On January 8, 1806, cold and tired, Pike and his men reached a British trading post at Red Cedar Lake—an outpost of the twelve-year-old North West Fur Company. Pike and his men enjoyed the hospitality of the proprietors, then abruptly ordered the British to lower their flag and pay customs duties for operating on United States lands.

As he left the post, Zebulon Pike vowed to complete his last major objective: to find and map the source of the Mississippi River. On February 1, 1806, believing he had reached his goal, Pike arrived at Leech Lake, another British fur post.

Leech Lake, Pike proclaimed in his journals, was the true headwater of the Mississippi River system. His discovery would have been

ZEBULON MONTGOMERY PIKE

PAINTING BY CHARLES WILLSON PEALE C.1792

Independence National Historical Park

a great achievement—but he was wrong. The source of the Mississippi is Lake Itasca, not far from Leech Lake. The error was corrected decades later.

During his stay at Leech Lake, Pike met with the Chippewas. The Indians agreed to relinquish the British flags, medals, and presents the fur traders had given them, and to refrain from drinking liquor (the United States officers hoped this would promote peaceful relations). The British agreed to pay duties on furs taken from what were now United States lands. In sparsely populated areas, however, residents took less notice of borders and absent landowners. After Pike left on February 18, the Chippewas retrieved their colorful British flags, medals, and presents, and the British resumed their normal activities.

Pike and his men arrived at the log cabins of his Little Falls winter camp on March 5. He waited for the river to thaw and returned without incident to St. Louis on April 30, 1806.

Pike's Mississippi expedition turned out to have been only partly successful. He had explored the area for the United States Government. He had made important maps for those who would follow him. And, he had obtained ownership of tracts of land that could be used for military posts. But the United States Senate failed to ratify the treaty he had made with the Sioux, and he hadn't reached the true source of the Mississippi. In addition, few of the chiefs took up Pike's invitations to journey to St. Louis and meet with General Wilkinson, the representative of the Great Chief of the East.

General Wilkinson, however, was rightfully impressed with Lieutenant Pike. Wilkinson immediately promoted Pike to captain and assigned him a much more rigorous exploring expedition.

President Jefferson had envisioned at least four expeditions into the lands of the new Louisiana Purchase. But Meriwether Lewis and

William Clark, the first explorers dispatched to the new region, had been gone for over two years now. Jefferson had received no word of their whereabouts for over a year. Most people assumed they were dead in some distant land.

A second expedition led by Captain Richard Sparks had set off up the Red River with scientists Thomas Freeman and Peter Custis. General Wilkinson had Pike in mind for a third such expedition into the West, but this one had a hidden agenda.

Pike's orders were to escort fifty-one Osage prisoners and a few chiefs who had paid visits to United States settlements back to their lands. From there, Pike was to try to negotiate peace between the Osages and their neighbors, the Pawnees. If he succeeded, the Captain was to explore the headwaters of the Arkansas and Red rivers, then return downstream on the Red to the Mississippi. If he could negotiate a treaty with the Comanches along the way, so much the better.

Wilkinson also gave Pike specific written orders concerning the Spanish. As Captain Pike's travels might take him close to the lands of New Spain, Wilkinson ordered: "should your route lead you near them, or should you fall in with any of their parties your conduct must be marked by circumspection and direction as may prevent alarm or conflict, as you will be held responsible for consequence."

These were his official orders. More than likely, Pike also had secret orders from the General. At the time, many people in the United States expected that, sooner or later, the country would go to war with Spain. General Wilkinson wanted to learn as much as possible about Spanish settlements, troop strength, trade routes, resources, and anything else that might help the United States.

The United States claimed that its border with New Spain extended along the Rio Grande; the Spanish maintained that the line lay farther north, along the Red River. General Wilkinson probably told Pike to observe and record as much as he could while exploring these border regions. If Pike were captured, it might be a way for him to see even more—Santa Fe, for instance, and other areas well within Spanish territory.

What few people (if any) knew was that James Wilkinson may have had ulterior motives for obtaining information on Spanish settlements and military posts. Later, Wilkinson and Aaron Burr were suspected of plotting to create a separate state in the West that could eventually conquer Mexico. Pike probably heard nothing of these rumored traitorous plans.

On July 15, 1806, twenty-seven-year-old Zebulon Pike left St. Louis with twenty-two men and the Osage warriors. Included under his command were fifteen men who he described as "A Dam'd set of rascals but very proper for such expeditions as I am engaged in." Lieutenant Wilkinson, an Army officer who also happened to be the General's son, accompanied the expedition, along with a surgeon, Dr. John Robinson, and an interpreter, Baronet Vasquez (called "Barney" by the men).

The group traveled for five weeks through humid, mosquito-infested lands to reach the Osage village. There, they released the Osage prisoners, traded the expedition's boats for horses, and set off overland, accompanied by thirty other Osage warriors and chiefs—the first exploring party into the Great Plains.

It took a week to travel ninety miles across rough terrain. Most of the men had "blistered and very sore feet." At the Pawnee village, Pike tried to bring about peace between the two tribes, and he may have had some success. The stop there also allowed the men to rest. They learned from traders that Lewis and Clark had returned from their incredible trip to the Pacific coast. Pike's journal betrays some jealousy of Lewis and Clark. He hoped to win fame and glory in much the same way they had, by achieving the objectives of his mission.

Pike wrote a letter to General Wilkinson from the Pawnee village and sent it by messenger back to St. Louis. In it, he updated the General on his progress, indicated where he was going next, and described what he would do if he met up with Spanish troops: "My instructions lead me into the Country of the Ietans—part of which is no Doubt claimed by Spain." The Ietans were Comanches. Pike indicated that if Spanish troops stopped him, he would claim that he was "uncertain as to his location."

This letter provides a key piece of evidence that Pike did indeed have secret orders to intentionally wander into land claimed by Spain. What Pike and almost no one else knew was that he was about to be betrayed. James Wilkinson, General of the Army, Governor of Louisiana Territory, conspirator with Aaron Burr, was also a paid agent of the Spanish. He was, in essence, a triple agent: paid as an officer in the United States Army, plotting traitorous acts, and receiving a pension from the Spanish in return for passing on information about border activities.

Even as Pike and his men traveled toward the Southwest, the Spanish knew of his mission. A large force of six hundred men and over two thousand horses and mules, under the command of Don Facundo Melgares, journeyed up to the headwaters of the Red River, looking for the American soldiers.

Pike, however, was nowhere to be seen. During October 1806, his expedition had crossed the Solomon, Saline, and Smoky Hill rivers and reached the big bend of the Arkansas River. Pike decided to send Lieutenant Wilkinson and five men back downstream to St. Louis with the journals, maps, and other documents they had compiled thus far. The lieutenant complained about the lack of food and ammunition provided the small party, but little food remained for anyone at that point.

Wilkinson and his men constructed two canoes out of cotton-wood trees and eventually made their way to the Mississippi River. The trip was difficult; three of the five men deserted before the party reached St. Louis.

Pike and the others traveled up the Arkansas. On November 15, 1806, they spotted the Rocky Mountains "looking like a small blue cloud." Two weeks of traveling brought them to the site of present-day Pueblo, Colorado. From there they could see a majestic peak rising into the sky. On impulse, Pike decided to climb this "grand peak." He set off, accompanied by Dr. Robinson and two other men.

The adventure started badly. The men wore only light cotton uniforms—they had not expected to encounter cold weather this far south—and the temperature had dropped to 22 degrees F. The party climbed for two and a half days and still only reached the summit of the first range of mountains. The peak looked as distant as before.

Pike estimated the mountain's summit to be eighteen thousand feet high. Actually, it is closer to fourteen thousand feet. It did eventually become known as Pikes Peak. But Zebulon Pike never climbed it. Cold, hungry, and surrounded by snow, the four unprepared men huddled together in a small cave for the night.

The next morning, Pike wrote in his journal:

27TH NOVEMBER, THURSDAY. -Arose hungry, dry, and extremely sore, from the inequality of the rocks, on which we had lain all night, but were amply compensated for toil by the sublimity of the prospects below. The unbounded prairie was overhung with clouds, which appeared like the ocean in a storm; wave piled on wave and foaming, whilst the sky was perfectly clear where we were. The summit of the Grand Peak which was entirely bare of vegetation and covered with snow, now appeared at the distance of fifteen or sixteen miles from us, and as high again as what we had ascended, and would have taken a whole day's march to arrive at its base, when I believe no human being could have ascended to its pinical.

That morning, the hungry men abandoned their climb and returned to a temporary camp where they had left supplies. Animals had destroyed most of their food. Instead of satisfying their hunger, the four men had to share one partridge and a piece of deer rib—their first meal in forty-eight hours.

When the adventurers got back to the Arkansas River, the expedition voyaged on to the mouth of Royal Gorge, sometimes known as the Grand Canyon of the Arkansas. The canyon was huge—sheer walls rose above the swirling waters. Just north of there, the party built a temporary shelter of logs. They left two men, most of the horses, and some supplies. The rest set off overland in search of the headwaters of the Red River.

But the Red River eluded them. After much wandering, they came across what Pike correctly guessed was the South Fork of the Platte River. The explorers eventually found another large river that seemed like it could only be the Red. They started downstream. Four weeks later, they found themselves back at the shelter at Royal Gorge, on the Arkansas River. For over a month, Pike had been leading his men in a giant circle.

Pike spent his birthday at the shelter. The realization that he had wasted so much time left him completely depressed: "This was my birthday, and most fervently did I hope never to pass another so miserably."

More depressing times lay ahead for the expedition. The party

~ PIKE'S 1805–1806 SEARCH FOR THE HEADWATERS OF THE
MISSISSIPPI RIVER.

~ PIKE'S 1806–1807 FAILED JOURNEY WEST TO THE RED
RIVER.

next attempted to cross the Sangre de Cristo range in winter. Snow and bitter cold stranded them high in the mountains, frostbitten, hungry, and sleep deprived. On Christmas Day, Pike managed to shoot several buffalo cows; the men devoured most of them. The soldiers moved on, but during an attempt to cross a patch of ice, many of their remaining horses fell. One slipped down a cliff and had to be shot.

The cold was brutal. The men cut up strips of blankets to wrap around their feet, but it didn't help. Before long, nine of them had frozen feet. The small party fought on through the mountains, their situation now desperate. Pike and Dr. Robinson—the only two without frostbite—went to look for game. That day, they shot and wounded a buffalo, but it ran off. The two men spent the night without food or shelter. The next day, January 19, 1807, they did kill a buffalo and they carried the meat back to camp. The men ate for the first time in four days.

Two of the privates could no longer walk. Frostbite sapped the little strength they had left. After much soul-searching and many tears, Pike left the men behind with only a few meager supplies.

The others headed southeast along the base of a mountain range, then climbed over a pass. Another two days' struggle through waist-deep snow left Pike feeling hopeless. The trip had reached its low point. Dr. Robinson killed another buffalo and the men filled their stomachs, but they had to leave behind another private with frozen limbs.

The party pushed on across another mountain pass. Two days later, they entered the San Luis Valley. The men must have thought they were in paradise after their weeks in the bitter cold of the mountains. They discovered sand dunes that looked like a "sea in a storm (except as to color)" (these later formed part of Great Sand Dunes National Park). In the middle of the valley, they found a gentle river that Pike identified as the Red River. He recorded the discovery in his journal entry of January 30. Pike was wrong again; it was the Rio Grande.

After moving onto a tributary of the river—the Conejos—Pike had some of the men construct a small fort. They built it of cottonwood logs and surrounded it with a moat by diverting water from the creek. The party was twelve miles southeast of present-day Alamosa, Colorado—deep inside Spanish territory. That didn't stop Pike from raising the American flag atop their fort.

The rest of the men went back to rescue the three soldiers left in the mountains. The first relief party brought back the solitary man abandoned closest to the San Luis Valley. His frostbitten legs improved on the way out, and he actually limped into the valley on his own feet.

The other two men hadn't fared as well. By the time the small relief party reached them, they could not even be carried. They sent the rescuers back with evidence of their desperate situation: pieces of gangrenous toe bones that had broken off their feet. Miraculously, those men survived too. Another rescue team managed to bring them back to the fort.

While the rescues went forward, Dr. Robinson left for Santa Fe—despite the fact that injured men needed his medical skills. He said he had to collect a debt owed an Illinois merchant by a person in Santa Fe. It was a strange explanation. When the Spanish governor questioned Robinson later, he reportedly claimed he had been traveling with a party of hunters.

There is other evidence that Dr. Robinson betrayed Pike and his men. Robinson is said to have asked the Spanish authorities to take him to Chihuahua, as he intended to become a Spanish citizen. And immediately after Robinson's meeting with the Spanish, the governor dispatched patrols to the San Luis Valley to find Pike and his men.

One of the Spanish patrols spotted the fort on February 26, 1807; soon, a larger force arrived to capture Pike's command. Despite their harrowing experiences, their journey of discovery had really only just begun; but General Wilkinson and the mysterious Dr. Robinson had ended it by betraying the explorers to the Spanish.

The local governor was convinced that Zebulon Pike and his men were spies. He didn't want to risk starting a war with the United States, so he had the prisoners escorted to Chihuahua. There, the authorities interrogated Pike for months, confiscating all his maps, journals, and notes. The Spanish finally released Pike. They sent him and some of his men under armed escort through Texas to Natchitoches, on the Louisiana border. The group arrived on June 30, 1807.

For unexplained reasons, the Spanish kept five of the men in prison in Mexico for two more years. A sixth, Sergeant William Meek, later killed an American private, Theodore Miller, while Meek was drunk and was held by the Spanish for fourteen years.

Under normal circumstances, Zebulon Pike would have returned from his expedition a national hero—an honor he had always craved. But the Aaron Burr conspiracy, and James Wilkinson's role in it, came to light before the Spanish freed Pike. Anyone associated with Wilkinson was branded a co-conspirator. As soon as he reappeared, Pike was drawn into the national inquiry and accused of treason.

Pike was exonerated—the government had no evidence that he was anything but a loyal, dedicated soldier who had followed his commander's orders, unaware of any political maneuvering. He may have accepted a questionable commission to travel along the Spanish border, but it appears that he was, in fact, truly lost on several occasions.

Once he had cleared his name, Pike wrote the report of his

expedition. It was a difficult task. Except for the few journals he sent back with Lieutenant Wilkinson, Pike no longer had any maps or notes. He did have an incredible memory, and he was able to reconstruct his journal records. He had also kept his eyes and ears open throughout his months in New Spain. He reported on Spanish customs, trade, settlements, military strength, transportation, and other aspects of life in the southern lands.

Pike's recall of events in the mountains turned out to have been even more amazing: his original papers were rediscovered in Mexican archives in 1907; nine years later, they were sent to the United States National Archives. The records matched his reconstructed entries very closely.

A year after his return from Mexico, Pike was promoted to Major. His report, published in 1810, gave the impression that the land between the Mississippi and the Rocky Mountains was a barren wasteland (it later came to be known as "The Great American Desert"): "The vast plains of the Western Hemisphere may become as celebrated as the sandy deserts of Africa." Pike concluded that most of the Great Plains was untillable and "best left to the wandering and uncivilized aborigines of the country."

Another explorer, Stephen Long, reinforced Pike's misperceptions of the Great Plains. Theirs would remain the prevailing opinion until John C. Frémont advised otherwise more than thirty years later. Pike's report did persuade some people to move to those barren lands. His notation on the presence of huge herds of buffalo along the southern Plains attracted hunters for decades.

Pike's report, *An Account of Expeditions to the Sources of the Mississippi and Through the Western Parts of Louisiana*, was eventually published in German, French, Dutch, and British editions. It brought him the fame that he had sought for so long.

Just two years later, Pike was promoted to Colonel of the fifteenth Infantry. When the United States went to war with the British, Pike was named brigadier general, in charge of twenty-five hundred men encamped near Lake Champlain. He was ordered to lead his men into battle to take Fort York (now Toronto) before his promotion became official. "You will hear of my fame or my death," he wrote in a letter. He foretold well. After the Americans charged and took the outer battery, the British commander blew up his powder magazine as his men retreated. General Zebulon Pike and fifty-one of his men were killed.

Pike was a man of dedication and perseverance. He explored vast tracts of the southern Great Plains, the eastern Rocky Mountains, and the upper Mississippi Valley, enduring many hardships. He had always dreamed of serving his country and achieving fame, and he succeeded in both. After his death, one of his contemporaries, General Whiting, noted, "Probably no officer in the Army was held in higher esteem."

Before he left for his final battle, Pike wrote a letter to his father.

I embark tomorrow in the fleet at Sackett's Harbor, at the head of a column of 1,500 choice troops, on a secret expedition. If success attends my steps, honor and glory await my name—if defeat, still shall it be said we died like brave men, and conferred honor, even in death, on the American name. ■

CHAPTER SIX

~ *The Great American Desert*

Stephen Long

W hen he entered the office of John C. Calhoun, the Secretary of War, Major Stephen Long was depressed. Long had waited years to lead a grand expedition into the West. In 1819, his chance had come: he was called on to lead the scientific portion of a grandiose expedition called the Yellowstone Expedition.

Now, almost as suddenly, it seemed that nothing would be salvaged from the unsuccessful, expensive disaster the expedition had become. Long had left his party of explorers and returned to Washington, D.C. this spring of 1820 in hopes that the secretary would approve a new plan—one that would allow Long to resurrect the scientific part of the Yellowstone Expedition and undertake a greater exploring trip than even Lewis and Clark's some fifteen years before.

Stephen Long urged Calhoun to approve a modified plan that would counteract the bad publicity the first part of the expedition had earned. Long accepted part of the blame for the failure of the mission thus far. He admitted mistakes in poor judgment and poor organization. Then he explained his new plan. He would take his party of soldiers and scientists westward across the Great Lakes, then down the St. Croix River to Fort St. Anthony (present-day Minneapolis). From there, they would travel to the Missouri River and on up to the headwaters of the Platte, Arkansas, and Red rivers. If Secretary Calhoun was agreeable, Major Long would explore as far as the Pacific Coast.

Calhoun's response was discouraging. The mood in Congress was ugly. The public was justifiably angry at the failure of the Yellowstone Expedition, and Congress was not anxious to authorize any more money for boondoggles.

As he left Calhoun's office, Stephen Long feared his chance for fame was slipping away. He immediately went to his quarters and wrote a letter—this time proposing an even more modest exploration, but one that would still explore new lands and would bring back valuable scientific knowledge. This expedition could be accomplished largely with the men at hand at a cost of only eight thousand dollars. It could be completed in four months.

As he waited for an answer from the War Department, Long had plenty of time to think back over the first thirty-five years of his life. He wondered whether all his hard work would ever result in that one great exploration—the kind that people associated with Meriwether Lewis, William Clark, and Zebulon Pike.

Many great explorers come from humble beginnings. Stephen Harriman Long was born in Hopkinton, New Hampshire, on December 30, 1784 to a barrel maker and his wife. His father, a Revolutionary War veteran, was a town selectman and tax collector who encouraged his son to study science and the classics.

Despite having only a modest formal education, Long was admitted to Dartmouth College when he was twenty-one years old. He excelled at his studies and was elected to Phi Beta Kappa. After graduation in 1809, Long taught school in New Hampshire, then took a job as a school principal in Germantown, Pennsylvania.

An opportunity arose in 1815 that Long found hard to resist. He received a letter of commission (sent to the wrong city, it had wandered in the mails for two months) appointing him a second lieutenant in the U.S. Army Corps of Engineers. He accepted. Long's status in the military rose quickly. He taught mathematics for a year at West Point, impressed his superiors, and received a promotion to major in 1816. Soon, he was surveying routes for the Baltimore and Ohio Railroad.

In 1817, Long helped survey parts of Illinois and the lower Arkansas River. The party mapped out a site at the mouth of the Poteau River to construct Fort Smith. On another surveying trip up the Mississippi and Wisconsin rivers, Long and his colleagues located a site for Fort St. Anthony, which would later become Minneapolis-St. Paul, Minnesota.

This was all good training for Long. Already skilled in mathematics and science, he soon became an accomplished surveyor and mapmaker as well. In addition, he had been tinkering with designs for special steamboats that could transport men and equipment up the Missouri River. His ideas were promoted through the ranks and eventually reached the attention of several people in the War Department—particularly the secretary, John C. Calhoun.

Calhoun had some rather grandiose plans for the West. He envisioned a series of frontier forts constructed much farther west than any before, even along the Yellowstone River. With such forts, Calhoun felt, the United States could demonstrate its strength to the Native

American tribes of the region and keep the British from using United States lands for their trapping and trading operations.

Calhoun took Long's steamboat idea and ran with it. Soon, he had authorized an eleven-hundred-person military force to travel up the Missouri under Colonel Henry Atkinson. Five steamboats would provide their transportation. Major Long would take a sixth steamboat with a small military and scientific party.

Calhoun's idea sounded good on paper, but the five military steamboats never made it past the mouth of the Kansas River. Long's plan for shallow-draft, specially designed steamboats had been scrapped in favor of hastily built, expensive, more conventional craft, which broke down. Stranded, Colonel Atkinson marched his men to a site near present-day Omaha, arriving in September 1819. The men built a fort and settled in for the winter.

Long, meanwhile, had left Pittsburgh on May 3, 1819, in a steamboat built to his original design. Within a week, the *Western Engineer* steamed quickly to Cincinnati, reaching St. Louis on June 9. Eventually, Long's boat made it farther upriver than the other boats, arriving at the new fort, Camp Missouri, on September 17, 1819.

The military base changed its name to Fort Atkinson, and later, Fort Calhoun; but it was as Fort Atkinson that it became infamous. During the winter of 1819–1820, more than a hundred of Atkinson's men died of scurvy. The Yellowstone Expedition, as it came to be known, had cost many lives without achieving anything.

Stephen Long was frustrated. For years, he had advocated combining military survey parties with scientific studies. Finally, he had an impressive team of scientists and artists organized and ready to go. They had spent a productive four and a half months together on their way from Pittsburgh. And now they could only sit and watch the Yellowstone Expedition end before it began.

STEPHEN LONG

PAINTING BY CHARLES WILLSON PEALE c.1819

Independence National Historical Park

Long's team, in addition to the officers, enlisted men, four members of the steamship crew, and two cabin boys, included twenty-one-year-old Titian Peale, the assistant naturalist, and thirty-five-year-old Thomas Say, an accomplished zoologist. Both would become nationally known in their fields. William Baldwin did double-duty as the group's physician and botanist, and Augustus Jessup served as its geologist. Samuel Seymour was the group's lead artist. Titian Peale had artistic talent as well and helped record impressions of the countryside and illustrate the plant and animal specimens. Two competent mapmakers added their abilities to Long's. And finally, Captain Thomas Biddle Jr. served as the expedition's journalist and kept the exploration records.

The *Western Engineer*'s journey from Pittsburgh to Camp Missouri was not without incident. Thomas Say's horses were stolen by Pawnees one day as the zoologist was collecting samples on shore. Say and Jessup both developed illnesses, which delayed the expedition. Dr. Baldwin himself became so ill that he was left behind in a Missouri town. He died there not long after, never having reached the western lands he'd hoped to explore.

At the end of the winter of 1820, Long was ready to press on, but the deaths of the soldiers encamped at Fort Atkinson made Congress cynical. The Yellowstone Expedition was left in limbo.

A somber Stephen Long, accompanied by Augustus Jessup, returned to the East in the spring of 1820. Long had another reason for making the lengthy trip—he married his fiancé in Philadelphia. Jessup had decided to quit the expedition. Unlike Long, Jessup was not in the military; he had signed on to make a trip in 1819 and it was now well into 1820.

Long also had lost Captain Thomas Biddle (a member of the prominent Biddle family of Philadelphia, he had received a brevet promotion to major during the War of 1812), who was to have maintained the official records of the trip. Biddle and Long suffered bitter conflicts in their short relationship. After only three months, Biddle joined Colonel Atkinson's command, having kept very few records for Long. Long had already arranged to replace Biddle with Captain John Bell.

Stephen Long waited five weeks after his meeting with Calhoun before receiving a decision. When it came, it wasn't exactly what he had envisioned.

Congress refused to invest any more money in anything to do with the Yellowstone Expedition. But it did endorse a smaller, less ambitious expedition—something like the one Long had proposed. A military detachment was to open a route from Fort St. Anthony to Fort Atkinson; meanwhile, Major Long could take his smaller scientific detachment west to the Rockies to find the sources of the Platte, Arkansas, and Red rivers. Science would be a major component of the expedition.

So far so good. The bad news was that Congress had granted them no additional funds—Long would have to make do with what he had. The scientists were eventually paid $2.20 per day, but they had to supply most of their own equipment. Despite the lack of sufficient pay, Calhoun insisted that the team produce quality maps and add to scientific knowledge. "You will enter in your journal, everything interesting in relation to soil, face of the country, water courses and productions, whether animal, vegetable, or mineral," instructed Calhoun. The secretary also attached a copy of Thomas Jefferson's instructions to Lewis and Clark, which he said contained "many valuable suggestions."

Because of the lack of supplies, Long's group would have to accomplish its goals as quickly as possible. The party received no extra funds, but was still expected to do everything. These were tall orders for an expedition that Stephen Long had estimated would cost at least eight thousand dollars more. But after all, Calhoun's reputation was at stake; the problems thus far had severely tarnished it.

Stephen Long rallied his spirits: here was still a chance to lead men into the wilds of the West on a grand expedition—one that could be mentioned in the same breath as that of Lewis and Clark.

Before he returned to his party's winter encampment along the Missouri, Long needed to fill the vacancies on his scientific team. He was fortunate to engage Dr. Edwin James to replace both Baldwin and Jessup. A physician and botanist, James would also serve as the group's geologist. And, he kept a personal journal during the trip— one that would ultimately prove invaluable.

With renewed enthusiasm, Long traveled with James to the Missouri River in the late spring of 1820, joining the others at Fort Atkinson. They outfitted themselves as best they could. The band of military men, surveyors, artists, and "scientific gentlemen" set off on June 6, 1820, leading a string of pack animals. One of the packs contained copies of Lewis and Clark's *Journals*, Alexander von Humboldt's *Personal Narrative of Travels to the Equinoctial Regions of America*, and maps compiled by explorers William Clark and Zebulon Pike. The crew of the *Western Explorer* bid the expedition farewell, intending to await their return.

The party stopped at a group of Pawnee villages early in the trip. They held councils with the chiefs and distributed presents. Like Lewis and Clark before him, Major Long hoped to establish peaceful relations with Native Americans; John C. Calhoun's instructions—"You will conciliate the Indians by kindness and presents"—also encouraged him to do so.

Artist Samuel Seymour immortalized the moment in several

careful drawings that still survive. It was an impressive sight: over five thousand Pawnee scattered among the villages, fields of corn and pumpkins, and six to eight thousand horses grazing in vast fields of grass.

From the Pawnee villages, the expedition headed south to the Platte River, arriving on June 22. The men continued westward for eight days, averaging twenty-five miles a day, before sighting the Rocky Mountains. Within a week, they had discovered an impressive mountain (they named it Longs Peak) and had partially accomplished their first objective—they reached the headwaters of the Platte River. The party camped near the site of present-day Denver on July 5.

Long's expedition then traveled along the upper part of the South Platte, but didn't fully explore the region. Instead, the party turned south and found the majestic peak that explorer Zebulon Pike had discovered years before. This time, a party of explorers (Dr. James and two other men) reached the top.

By late July, the party had arrived at the Arkansas River near present-day Pueblo, Colorado. Like Pike and his fellow explorers, Long's party journeyed up the Arkansas to Royal Gorge, an impressive walled canyon. They mapped, surveyed, and collected as they went. Beyond the gorge, travel became too difficult, and the men turned back. They had reached the Arkansas—another of their objectives—but had failed to explore the headwaters as Calhoun had instructed.

Here, Stephen Long decided to divide the exploring party. Captain Bell, Thomas Say (the zoologist), Samuel Seymour (the artist), Lieutenant Swift, five privates, and three French guides headed down the Arkansas River. They took with them most of the heavy supplies and most of the pack animals, along with the journals, notes, and specimens of plants and animals the party had on hand. Bell intended

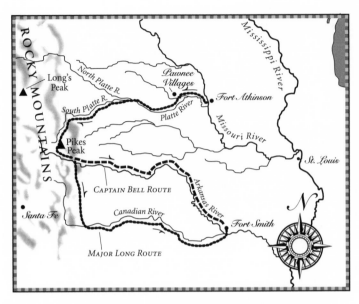

~ Long's 1819–1820 western expedition
and search for the Red River.

to explore the Arkansas and then wait at Fort Smith for Long and the
rest of the party.

Captain Bell's party looked ragged as it set off. Many of the horses
were weak and emaciated, and the men didn't look much better. The
food they took with them was less than a modest supply: three-quar-
ters of a pound of coffee, an ounce of tea, half a pound of sugar, three
pecks of cornmeal, nine pints of corn, twelve pounds of biscuits, five
pints of whiskey, and four bottles of lemon acid.

Major Long, meanwhile, would take Titian Peale, Dr. James, and
seven soldiers south to try and find the headwaters of the Red River.
By now, the men were thoroughly hungry and exhausted. Long drove
them relentlessly. He hurried them through their tasks, determined
not to return to the East without accomplishing Calhoun's objectives,
and focused on obtaining the maximum scientific contribution.

Inconsistent leadership was one of Long's shortcomings. He was alternately a disciplinarian and a sensitive commander, which sometimes confused the men. He had also argued with Captain Bell.

The two groups parted company on July 24, 1820. Long and his men crossed the Purgatory River, then the Cimarron. Finally, they found a river flowing to the southeast that the major concluded must be the Red River. But Long did not head upstream to explore the water's upper reaches, as he had hoped to and as Calhoun had instructed; instead he turned downstream. He and all of his men were dragging. The news that they had reached the Red River and were now heading home lifted the men's spirits. They began the interminable ride along the river's banks, sometimes crossing the river to travel on easier terrain.

Traveling was still difficult. Constantly out of food, plagued by the heat, ticks, and mosquitoes, the party frequently encountered bands of Kiowas and Comanches. Sometimes tempers flared, but no single incident was tragic.

Temperatures soared to over 100 degrees F. The land was desolate and barren. The men could not even find firewood. They resorted to using buffalo chips for their cooking fires. Water fit for drinking was scarce along the tea-colored Red River. The horses could find little grass. The number of scientific collections and observations declined; that sort of activity didn't seem as important any more.

On July 27, the men were extremely hungry. Long sent out a small party of hunters. They managed to shoot a young buffalo, but the animal ran off. They followed its tracks for some time, then came upon a chilling sight: the wounded buffalo was surrounded by a pack of wolves as hungry as the men. The men had to drive off the wolves before they could take the buffalo meat back to camp. The party heartily welcomed their first substantial meal in days and stayed up much of the night eating second, third, and even fourth helpings of the meat.

By now, Long and his men had only one goal: to get to Fort Smith. Horses went lame on the rough terrain; their energy drained hourly. No one felt nourished. One day, a hunter might kill a deer, then for many days there would be nothing. Another day, they shot and killed a wild horse. They thankfully accepted whatever they could get.

The naturalists occasionally encountered something unusual, and they still managed to stop and collect, measure, or draw a specimen. Resting from their travels one day, the party watched intently as a huge brown centipede, some eight inches long, crept along near them.

The explorers encountered Native American tribes more and more often. Many of the Indians tried to steal horses and other supplies; the major and his men had to be constantly on guard. Long followed the example of Lewis and Clark and stood up to any threat, even against superior numbers. This approach almost always worked to fend off attack.

Captain Bell's group, meanwhile, was experiencing many of the same difficulties on the Arkansas River. The men were always hungry. They managed to survive on half a cup of cornmeal a day and any game they could find. By August 21, the cornmeal was gone. The men shot and shared a skunk for their meal.

Bell met fewer Indians, but suffered a serious setback from within his party. On the morning of August 31, about halfway to Fort Smith, the captain awoke to find that three of his soldiers had deserted, taking with them the three best horses and many of the supplies. Worse, the men had stolen most of the journals and the other reports that Stephen Long and the scientific team had spent so many weeks compiling. These included daily diaries as well as countless scientific notebooks. Thomas Say alone lost five notebooks. Most records of the expedition's lengthy journey were now lost.

The party had only dying horses left and virtually no food. There was no game in sight. Some of the men could no longer walk. The expedition's two dogs, Buck and Caesar, did die, from a combination of starvation and exhaustion. Had it not been for the kindness of a passing hunting party of Osage Indians, the men, too, might have been lost. The Osages gave the explorers what little food they had; it was enough to keep the travelers going.

Long's party, meanwhile, found an abandoned log canoe, loaded it with supplies, and pushed, pulled, and dragged it downstream. The next day, September 1, 1820, Stephen Long recorded his longitude and latitude. He knew he had been traveling eastward, but he was surprised to find himself much farther north than he had supposed. On September 10, he found out why: the river he had led his group down was the Canadian, a tributary of the Arkansas. They had never even seen the Red River.

Like Zebulon Pike, who had mistaken the Rio Grande for the Red, Long had failed to reach his objective. He wrote in his journal of his "Disappointment and chagrin" at having misidentified the Canadian as the Red River. But Native Americans along his route had assured Long that he was on the Red River. Long had not realized that some tribes called various rivers "red" because of the color of the water.

The party fought its way through a canebrake and dense river bottom vegetation and arrived, exhausted, at the confluence of the Canadian and the Arkansas rivers. The men tried to sleep, though heavy rains drenched them that night. The next day, a chance encounter with some travelers along an old trail revealed that Bell and his men had passed down that same trail just five days before. They knew now that they were close. Their spirits rose.

On September 13, the haggard men saw Fort Smith on the opposite bank and felt a tremendous relief. The commander of the post invited them to a hearty meal, unlike anything they had eaten for months: vegetables, meat, bread, and sweet potatoes. The commandant warned the men that the food might upset their shrunken stomachs, but it did little good. Long and his men ate like the starved creatures they were—and most of them became quite sick.

Long sent a brief written report to Secretary Calhoun. He and his men made their way, in separate groups, to the Missouri, where they rejoined the *Western Engineer*. The crew had been waiting for weeks, fearing that the explorers might have perished somewhere in the wilderness. The steamboat traveled up the Ohio River. Most of the explorers left the boat after that to make their way to the East Coast by other means.

The expedition of 1819–1820 was Stephen Long's most important, but he wasn't through exploring. He proposed another expedition to the West, but lack of funds quashed the idea. Orders for a new expedition came from John C. Calhoun, by way of the Chief of Engineers, Colonel Alexander Macomb. Long was to travel up the Mississippi to Fort St. Anthony (later known as Fort Snelling, now St. Paul, Minnesota), then proceed to the mouth of the Minnesota River. From there, he would explore the Red River of the North to the 49th Parallel, head toward Lake Superior, and make his way home. Again, Calhoun wanted records of natural resources along the way.

Major Long almost didn't make the trip. Unhappy that the accomplishments of his larger expedition had been somewhat ignored, and wanting to be near his wife, he had applied for a civil engineering position in Virginia. But when the new commission arrived, he reconsidered. The Army Corps of Engineers had been Stephen Long's life, and the idea of leading an expedition to the North was exciting. Many veterans and experienced scientists from the first expedition, such as Thomas Say and Samuel Seymour, were interested in going.

Long enticed William Keating, a very competent geologist, and James Calhoun, a mapmaker, to come, too. In the end, Long gave up his Virginia plans.

Another man joined the group at Fort St. Anthony: an Italian adventurer named Giacomo Beltrami. Beltrami carried a bright red umbrella wherever he went. He and Long did not hit it off. Beltrami called the major pompous and ill-mannered, even "disgusting." Long referred to the Italian as an "amateur traveler." They fought constantly, and Beltrami eventually left the expedition. Later, when his guides deserted, Beltrami found himself stranded in the wilds without the faintest idea of how to paddle a canoe. He finally managed to make his way alone and eventually returned to Italy with an important collection of Native American artifacts that he used to open a museum.

Long's northern expedition left Philadelphia on April 30, 1823 and reached Fort Dearborn, near present-day Chicago, a little over a month later. Traveling conditions were miserable and Long hoped that the remainder of the trip would be better. From the southern end of Lake Michigan, the party traveled to Fort St. Anthony, then took the Red River of the north northward.

Their only openly hostile encounter with Native Americans occurred soon afterward. Some of the men, sitting over an elk they had killed, were surrounded by a band of Sioux. The Sioux threatened to take the explorers' horses. The warriors outnumbered Long and his men by almost three to one. Weapons were raised on both sides, but the Sioux eventually backed down.

Long also had problems with a lack of discipline among his men. Once, several of them got drunk and refused to follow orders. Long drew a pistol and they changed their minds. One man later deserted, taking supplies and causing the others to go hungry.

Instead of following his orders to explore the 49th Parallel eastward, Long actually traveled into Canada. The direct line of the 49th Parallel followed marshes and bogs, while rivers to the north allowed the men to use canoes. By September 15, 1823, they had reached the shores of Lake Superior.

On September 27, the party arrived at Sault Ste. Marie. They continued on to Detroit, Lake Erie, Buffalo, and finally, Rochester, New York. On October 27, Major Long returned to Philadelphia. He had explored, mapped, and collected for six months, and had traveled over 4,500 miles.

This time, Congress and the public did take notice. Stephen Long became a household name.

Later in his life, Long made surveys for the railroad, directed the dredging of rivers, constructed hospitals, and worked as an engineer on New York's harbor defenses. He wrote books on railroad and bridge construction. After covering 26,000 miles during five expeditions, he retired at the age of seventy-nine.

Long's expedition across the Great Plains remained the crowning achievement of his career. Despite difficult traveling and an almost constant battle with hunger, and despite the theft of many of the expedition's journals, the scientific and mapping accomplishments of the party were truly impressive.

Long's team brought back more than sixty skins of new or unusual animal species and thousands of insect specimens—probably seven to eight hundred of which had been unknown to science. In addition, they described between 140 and 500 new plant species. Thomas Say discovered thirteen birds, twelve reptiles and amphibians, and various other invertebrates. Say and Edwin James were the first to identify, using correct scientific names, many plants and animals of the Great Plains. Among the strange animals first seen on the expedition were the coyote, the prairie gray wolf, several types of squirrels and bats, the prairie rattlesnake, the mule deer, the band-tailed pigeon, the blue grouse, and the blue racer.

Unfortunately, no one knows the exact number of new species Long's expedition described, or even the number of specimens they brought back; almost all the animal and insect specimens have been lost. P.T. Barnum's Museum, in New York, displayed some, but the museum and specimens were destroyed in a fire in 1865. Many of the remaining specimens decomposed. Some of the plants survived in the New York Botanical Garden, and a few animal specimens were saved by the Harvard Museum of Comparative Zoology.

Long's maps were extremely valuable. They remained the standard references until John C. Frémont's surveying trips some twenty years later.

The explorers did manage to write a full report of the expedition, despite the missing journals. Stephen Long, Thomas Say, and Edwin James had all kept accounts of various sorts. Long and the scientists sat in an office provided by the government and pooled their information. They had to buy their own paper and other supplies for the report. James and Say, as nonmembers of the military, did receive a small per diem while they worked. Captain Bell's journal, lost before the others could make use of it, was actually rediscovered in 1932.

Edwin James did most of the writing, consolidating the notes of the others. The result, supplemented by scientific notes and maps, with illustrations by Samuel Seymour, was a two-volume compilation of the 1819–1820 expedition: *Account of an Expedition From Pittsburgh to the Rocky Mountains*. Long was at a disadvantage in publicizing it: the Secretary of War authorized the printing of only a few dozen copies at government expense. Long had to publish most copies privately. The War Department did pay for printing the maps. The account became a classic of exploration literature; it is still popular.

The write-up of the Great Lakes expedition took place under similar arrangements. Long, Keating, Say, and Seymour all collaborated, working out of an office in Philadelphia. The non-military people received two dollars a day from the government. Keating wrote the report, entitling it *Narrative of an Expedition to the Source of St. Peter's River, Lake Winnepeek, Lake of the Woods, Et Cetera.* The northern expedition also lost many of its scientific specimens, this time during transit. The team still managed to describe dozens of new species it had discovered. The two volumes, published in December 1824, never gained the renown of the first report.

Sometimes forgotten are the extensive notes that Long and the others made about Native Americans. Long even produced the first dictionary of Native American sign language. It was rudimentary, but represented an important first attempt.

When Stephen Long first explored the West, many Americans had a very parochial view of the world. After the account of the 1819–1820 expedition came out, a reporter confessed to Dr. James his surprise that the scientist had actually met wild Indians—they were such a curiosity. The man was also astounded, James revealed, that the Native Americans were "ignorant, not only of the existence of the People of the United States, but of the existence of a race of White People."

Of all Stephen Long's legacies, perhaps the most potent was his description of the Great Plains of the United States. He had crisscrossed hundreds of miles of it, had suffered from the heat and the insects, and had discovered its lack of plenty: he and his men had nearly starved. Unimpressed with the "barrenness" of the land, he coined the phrase "The Great American Desert."

Long described the area as the "haunt of the bison and jackal." The "sole monarch" of the Great Plains was "the prickly pear, its chief inhabitant the horned frog." The eastern slope of the Rockies, he said, bore "a manifest resemblance to the deserts of Siberia," with huge herds of buffalo feeding on vast tracts of grass. Others in the party shared Long's view. Captain Bell called the Great Plains "a dusty plain of sand and gravel, barren as the deserts of Arabia." Dr. James thought it must be an extension of the "Mexican desert."

"In regard to this extensive section of the country," Long concluded, "I do not hesitate in giving the opinion, that it is almost wholly unfit for cultivation, and of course, uninhabitable by a people depending upon agriculture for their subsistence." He felt the Great Plains "would serve as a barrier to prevent too great an extension of our population westward." When the popular writer Washington Irving wrote his novel, *Astoria*, in 1836, he used the Long report to picture the desolate plains.

These descriptions had a profound influence on the United States. Long had said the plains were fit only for Indian tribes. Within five years of his report, the government instituted a national policy of transporting Native Americans of the east to these otherwise "inhospitable" lands between the Rockies and the Mississippi River.

The public's perception relied on Long's description of the Great Plains as unfit for farming or settlement. Thousands of immigrants bypassed the plains, pushing on to the more promising lands of Oregon and California. Not until twenty years later, when John C. Frémont traveled the plains and came to a very different conclusion, did the Great American Desert become a destination for settlers.

Stephen Long died in 1864 at the age of eighty. The reversal of his predictions on western settlement probably surprised him. He truly didn't think much of the Great Plains as a place to live—just crossing it had been an ordeal. ■

CHAPTER SEVEN

~ *The Toughest Man Alive*

Jedediah Smith

*A*n advertisement caught Jed Smith's eye. The enticing notice in the *Missouri Gazette and Public Advertiser* of Wednesday, February 13, 1822, offered employment for one hundred "young men of enterprise." These men would have the opportunity to "ascend the Missouri River to its source," a job that would take one, two, or three years. The notice was signed "Wm. H. Ashley."

Young and green, Jedediah Strong Smith seized the moment. He looked up Ashley and signed on. Smith had little idea of what might lie ahead; had he known, his decision would likely have been the same. He was about to embark on a career as a fur trapper, trader, and explorer. He would become a most unusual mountain man, bringing a unique lifestyle to a profession known for hard living.

Smith was a deeply religious man. He carried his Bible with him wherever he traveled, and he was fond of singing gospel songs while riding across desolate territory. Loyal to his Methodist upbringing, he didn't smoke or curse, and he resisted the temptations of Indian women in the mountains. Smith's behavior was unheard of among the fraternity of mountain men. To confuse the other trappers even more, Jedediah Smith was clean-shaven and he bathed regularly, even using soap.

But no one questioned Jedediah Smith's bravery, determination, and leadership. In many eyes, Smith was the toughest man alive.

Once, while traveling in the Black Hills with several companions, Smith was surprised by a grizzly bear. The animal leaped out of a thicket, knocked Smith off his horse, and grabbed him by the head. When the skirmish was over, several of Smith's ribs were broken and his scalp was laid open to the bone. The bear's teeth had left a white streak in their path. One of Smith's ears was dangling from the side of his head, nearly torn off.

Smith's companions were horrified—they had little hope of his survival. But he remained calm. He asked for some cool water, then had a fellow trapper, James Clyman, dress the wounds. Clyman cut away some of Smith's blood-soaked hair, but didn't think he could do more. Smith would hear none of it. He ordered Clyman to get needle and thread from his saddlebags, then he calmly explained how to sew his scalp back in place.

Clyman said that he did the best he could: "I told him I could do nothing for his Eare." Smith thought otherwise. He had his friend sew the mangled ear back onto his head. Then, he took a long drink of water, mounted his horse, and returned to their small camp in the hills. Ten days later, Jedediah Smith felt fit for more exploring—and off he went.

Smith was a man with plenty of sand. He became the greatest explorer of his day, covering more territory on foot and on horseback than anyone in that era.

≈ ≈ ≈

Jedediah Smith was a New Yorker, born in 1799 in what later became Bainbridge, a small town in Chenango County. Unlike many of the men who eventually migrated to the beaver waters of the Rocky Mountains, Smith was relatively well educated. A family friend—town doctor, Titus Simons—tutored him, and Smith never forgot his mentor. Smith became a lifelong reader and letter writer.

When he was a teenager, Smith worked as a clerk on the ships that traveled around Lake Erie. He had always dreamed of the Far West, ever since he had read an edited version of Lewis and Clark's journals. Before long, he headed to St. Louis. He was twenty-three years old.

William Ashley, one of the fur trade's important entrepreneurs, took a chance on the young man. Along with several other men who would soon become well known in the Rocky Mountain fur trade, Smith headed upriver under Ashley's patronage. In the spring of 1822, the group reached the headwaters of the Yellowstone River.

The following year, Ashley advertised for another group of enterprising young men. The second expedition traveled upstream to join the first. They left St. Louis in two keelboats, the *Yellowstone Packet* and the *Rocky Mountains*, on April 3, 1823.

At the time, Smith was still upriver with Ashley's field captain, Andrew Henry. Indians had stolen some fifty of their horses. Lack of transport hampered Henry's operation; the trappers couldn't move far from the fort. Somewhat desperate, Henry sent Smith down the Missouri in a canoe to contact Ashley and urge him to buy horses from the Sioux or the Arikara ("Rees," as the traders called them). Smith really caught Ashley's eye this time.

Smith met up with Ashley on the river in late May of 1823, just before the boat party reached the Arikara villages near the mouth of the Grand River. Once he learned of Henry's predicament, Ashley decided to stop and barter with the Arikara. It turned out to be a fatal decision.

The Missouri River passed the Arikara village in a long expanse of exposed water. If the Arikara were not feeling peaceful, the spot was a dangerous one for any traveler. Taking advantage of their situation, the Rees had built a breastwork of timber at the end of a sand bar opposite some high ground on the far bank.

The two keelboats carrying Smith and Ashley's party arrived at the village. After long negotiations, the Arikara agreed to sell Ashley nineteen horses and two hundred buffalo robes. The next morning, they reneged on the bargain; the Arikara said they would not sell unless they received guns and ammunition. The tribe was apparently still angry about a previous encounter with white traders.

The situation quickly turned ugly. Some six hundred warriors, most of them armed with old London fuzils, the rest with bows and arrows, attacked the expedition. The trappers were caught in the open. Many of the horses they had just acquired were killed during the battle. Twelve men died and eleven others were wounded. Two of the wounded later died. In the worst disaster in the history of the fur trade, Ashley had lost one-sixth of his company and goods worth over $2,200.

Ashley ordered a retreat downstream. When he asked the party to try advancing upriver again toward Henry's fort, the men refused— all except Smith. Not only had the young man showed bravery in battle, he volunteered to travel overland to reach Andrew Henry.

Out of disaster, a mountain man and successful businessman was born. By 1825, Smith would be one of Ashley's partners.

Between 1823 and 1825, however, Smith continued to work for Ashley as a fur trapper. Smith began to explore extensively, always searching for beaver and better trapping. The grizzly bear attack in the Black Hills only briefly delayed his wandering. Smith's wounds eventually healed, but the sewn-up scalp left him with a partial squint and a deformed ear. He took to wearing his hair long to hide his ear. This only added to his reputation.

Smith and his fellow trappers traveled from the Black Hills to the Powder River and on to the Bighorn Basin. They overwintered at a Crow village in the Wind River Valley. The white men joined the Crows on several hunts; Smith estimated they killed over a thousand buffalo that year.

In the spring, the trappers tried to leave the valley and cross the mountains at Union Pass, but deep snows blocked their route. They returned to the Crow village and learned of another pass. Traveling along the Popo Agie River and through a blizzard, the men finally reached the Continental Divide at South Pass in present-day Wyoming. Their crossing was an important event in American history. Another fur trapper, Robert Stuart, had traveled over South Pass years before—going from west to east—but the route had been largely forgotten. Smith "rediscovered" the pass and recorded its relatively gentle approach from the east. In decades to come, thousands of emigrants would take Smith's route in their westward travels.

After more exploring and trapping as Ashley's employee, Jedediah Smith took a major step in his personal career. At the summer Rendezvous of 1826, Smith formed a partnership with fellow trappers William Sublette and David Jackson. Together, they bought out William Ashley.

Smith drew up a lengthy contract. He and his partners agreed to pay William Ashley sixteen thousand dollars for Ashley's operation. They would settle their debt either in beaver pelts at the next year's Rendezvous or by paying Ashley a commission on pelts taken to St. Louis.

JEDEDIAH SMITH
Kansas State Historical Society

Ashley, in turn, agreed to provide the partners seven to fifteen thousand dollars in supplies at the 1827 Rendezvous. Buying Ashley's business was a gamble for the new partners. Ashley knew that the trade end of the fur business was much more lucrative and less risky than the fur-trapping part.

The deal was made at the 1826 Rendevous. The Rendezvous, initiated in 1825, was a fur-trading event that took place every year for sixteen years, until 1841. Traders set up camp, bought furs, and sold whiskey and supplies to trappers in one long drunken celebration. Beaver pelts, which sold for six to eight dollars in St. Louis, brought two to four dollars at the Rendezvous. But trappers gained by avoiding the long trip to the city. A good trapper might bring three or four hundred pelts to the Rendezvous. In 1825, Smith brought in 668.

The traders at the Rendezvous made most of their profit in trade goods. Whiskey that traders purchased for thirty cents a gallon in St. Louis sold for three dollars a pint in the mountains. Tobacco or coffee, normally ten cents a pound, brought two dollars a pound. Trade goods used by trappers to ensure safe passage through tribal lands—hawks bells, mirrors, cloth, knives—had a two-thousand-percent markup. Trappers often spent their entire season's earnings in one month of whiskey, women, and good times.

The fur trade was brisk, and the new partnership worked quite well the first year. David Jackson served as field captain—keeping trappers in the field—while William Sublette took an exploring party north, and Jedediah Smith took another party to look for beaver in the south.

Smith and his party left Cache Lake in the fall of 1826 and traveled south to the Great Salt Lake, exploring parts of the shoreline. They proved the lake of salty water had no connection to the Pacific Ocean, contrary to an assumption once made by mountain man Jim Bridger.

From there, the group entered Ute territory. It didn't look like beaver country, but no white man had travelled these parts. Smith and his trappers never knew whether they might find lush vegetation over the next ridge, with beavers swimming in valleys full of water. As it turned out, they didn't. The Utes were friendly enough when Smith gave them a number of gifts: red ribbon, a razor, ten awls, two knives, a pound of powder, and some lead balls, arrow points, and some tobacco. The Indians could not tell Smith much about the desert to the south, though.

Neither could the Paiutes. Smith described the tribe as extremely poor; they were people who grew corn and pumpkins and would "eat anything." He traded with them for a carved pipe made of a greenish marble; he planned to give the pipe to explorer William Clark for his museum of Indian "curiosities."

The weather had turned incredibly hot and the men and horses were dragging. Even the beautiful scenery (they were crossing an area that later became part of Zion National Park) didn't raise their spirits much. South of present-day St. George, Utah, Smith said he "learned what it was to do without food." Game was almost nonexistent and fresh water became scarce. It often took two days to get from one water hole to the next.

By the time the party reached the Colorado River, their horses were dying. The starved men were forced to eat the shriveled, blackened flesh of their animals. The heat was unbearable; the chocolate-colored waters of the Colorado brought little relief. When the expedition left the river, more than half of the horses had died and the men were traveling on foot.

Finally, the party emerged from the Black Mountains, only to gaze on one of the most barren furnaces of the Southwest—the Mojave Desert. The hospitality of the Mojave Indians saved the travelers. The

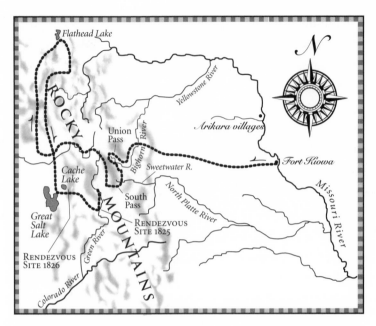

~ Smith's first fur-trapping expedition from
Fort Kiowa west to the Rocky Mountains.

Mojaves were extremely poor. Men and women both wore skirts made
of grass. They grew melons and a few vegetables in their gardens. Smith
and his men rested with the Mojaves for fifteen days.

The tribe told Smith about an old Indian trail that led across the
desert. Smith believed them—the village possessed things that could
only have come from traders in the west. He decided to keep moving
west. He didn't want to return to the Rockies the way he had come,
and the Mojaves assured him that the Spanish missions of California
were not far away. Smith and his men ventured into the desert with
two guides.

Everything is relative. "Not very far" took fifteen days to cross.
The party tried to follow the Mojave River westward, but it kept

disappearing into the desert soil. Jedediah named it the "Inconstant River." The men suffered from extreme heat and terrible thirst, but they made it to California. Smith and his companions were the first travelers from the United States to cross the Southwest overland via the Mojave Desert.

After the desert, the San Bernardino valleys (and, later, the area around the San Gabriel Mission) seemed like paradise. Sheep, cattle, and horses grazed on the green banks of gentle streams. The exhausted men were surprised to see two friars coming forward to greet them. The *padres* had a cow slaughtered, cooked, and served with cornmeal to the starving men. Smith never forgot their thoughtfulness.

In late November 1826, the friars escorted the men to Mission San Gabriel. There, Smith ran into trouble. California was Spanish territory and Smith and his men were illegal immigrants. The authorities took Smith to the governor, José Echeandìa, in San Diego, for questioning. Despite his harrowing journey to California, Smith couldn't convince the governor of the truth, that "I was only a hunter & that Dire necessity had driven me here."

The unsympathetic Spanish had little understanding of beaver trapping. In their report, they wrote the nearest thing to "trapper" they knew: Smith was a *pescador*—a fisherman. He remained under house arrest in San Diego until January 1827. Fortunately, the captains of three American merchant ships anchored in the bay vouched for Smith. The Spanish let him and his men go—on the condition that they leave California by the same route that had brought them there.

Despite his promise, Smith had no intention of crossing the Mojave Desert again. He took his men northward across the Tehachapi Mountains and into the San Joaquin Valley. They found a land full of contrasts—alkali flats, tule marshes, wildflowers, arid desert, and foothill valleys full of streams and game. The men trapped their way northward along the western slopes of the Sierra Nevada. When they reached the American River, near present-day Sacramento, their horses were packing over fifteen hundred pounds of beaver pelts.

In May 1827, after a period of rest, the trappers tried to head due east over the Sierra Nevada. Five horses died in the heavy snows. The party was forced to retreat some seventy-five miles back to the Stanislaus River. A short time later, Smith took two men, Robert Evans and Silas Gobel, and tried crossing the Sierras again. This time they made it, traveling over Ebbetts Pass.

Eleven men remained at the Stanislaus. They built log cabins and set about trapping until Smith's return. He had promised to bring back supplies within four months. Soon after Smith's departure, a detachment of Spanish soldiers arrived at the Stanislaus. The authorities had heard that Smith had violated his agreement and was still in California. But he was gone. The soldiers, thwarted in their mission, allowed the men to remain in their mountain camp. They seemed to present little threat, and would likely be gone when the mountain snows melted.

Smith, Evans, and Gobel suffered a more difficult fate. They lost two horses and a mule, but after eight days, they and the four remaining animals emerged on the eastern side of the Sierras. Smith didn't know what lay ahead, but the view was not promising. Before them, as far as they could see, was a desolate land. It was later called the Great Basin.

Crossing the Great Basin was an ordeal. One by one, the horses died or had to be killed in order for the men to survive. Their water was soon gone. In desperation, they ate the flesh and drank the blood of their dead horses. On June 25, Robert Evans collapsed from thirst and exhaustion. After much soul-searching, the other two decided to

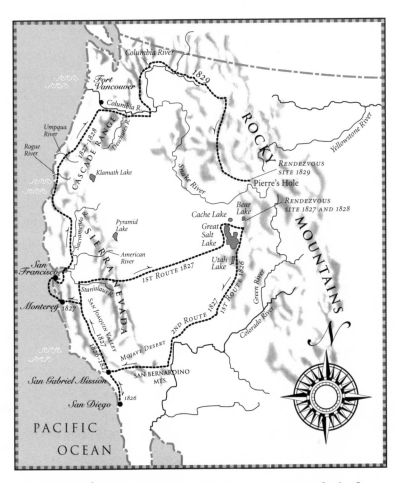

~ SMITH'S FUR-TRAPPING EXPEDITIONS OF 1826, 1827,
AND 1828, INCLUDING HIS DESERT ADVENTURES
AND ARRESTS BY THE SPANISH.

go on without him. Smith wrote in his diary, "We could do no good by remaining to die with him."

Then their luck turned. Three miles after leaving Evans, Smith and Gobel found a small water hole. They drank their fill, and Smith filled a container with water. He put a piece of horse meat inside and hurried back to Evans. Smith later wrote, "Putting the kettle to his mouth he did not take it away until he had drank all of the water, of which there was at least 4 or 5 quarts and then asked me why I had not brought more."

All three survived. The water hole was within sight of the Great Salt Lake. In another of western history's great feats of human endurance, the men had been the first to cross the Great Basin, covering over a thousand miles, much of it on foot. On July 3, they staggered into Bear Lake, near the present-day border between Idaho and Utah, for the Rendezvous of 1827. Their arrival shocked their fellow mountain men. "My arrival caused considerable bustle in camp," Smith wrote, "for myself and party had been given up for lost." The trappers fired off a small cannon to celebrate. They had been firing the cannon for weeks, and now they even had a reason to do it.

While Smith had been away, his partners had done well. They had paid their debt to William Ashley, who advanced them supplies for the coming year.

But Smith could not think about trapping; he had other priorities. His promise to the men at the Stanislaus River must be kept. Just ten days after arriving at the Rendezvous, Smith gathered supplies, recruited eighteen men and two of their Native American wives, and again headed south. Before he left, he wrote a letter to William Clark, the famous explorer, now Superintendent of Indian Affairs for the upper Missouri and Mississippi rivers. Smith described his journey to California and included notes on some of the tribes that he had encountered en route.

Smith revisited many of the same Indian villages in the next few weeks as he retraced his previous route south to the Colorado River. The most direct route, west across the Great Basin and the Sierras, had almost killed him before. Smith had no desire to see those lands again, even if avoiding them meant recrossing the arid lands to the southwest.

The trip went tolerably until they reached the Mojave. Their reception by the Mojave Indians was far less hospitable this time.

Smith had fashioned some makeshift rafts to ferry supplies across the Colorado River. The Indians waited to make their move until the trappers were most vulnerable. Smith and eight of the men had almost reached the far shore with some of the supplies when the Mojaves attacked. They killed all ten men waiting on the eastern river bank and took the two Indian wives of the trappers captive.

Smith and the others, stunned and helpless, could only watch. Finally, they ran for cover and dug in, thinking they, too, would die along the banks of the Colorado. The men made spears from cottonwood branches, tying their knives to the ends of the poles. The Mojaves attacked again, but Smith's men killed two of the warriors and the rest lost interest. One of the trappers was wounded in the second attack.

Eventually, the nine survivors were able to slip away into the Mojave Desert. They now had to travel on foot, virtually without supplies. They had five rifles, a little ammunition, and only fifteen pounds of dried meat between them and starvation—the Mojaves had taken everything else.

Smith wondered at the change in the Mojaves, who so recently had sheltered his men and fed them freshly grown melons. Apparently, a recent incident with traders had caused them to be wary of all travelers, even those who had peacefully entered their village a short time before.

The odds were against the Americans making it across the desert. They had no horses and little food or water. One of their number was wounded—unable to walk without help. And they were relying on Jedediah Smith's memory of an unmarked desert trail.

Fortunately, another band of Indians befriended Smith's party and traded them some horses. At a village the travelers passed through, Smith traded for more horses. But the journey was still difficult. Summer was at its height, and Smith kept losing the old trail. It was late August before they reached the Spanish settlements at San Gabriel.

Delaying at the Mission only long enough for his men to recover, Smith hurried northward and arrived at the Stanislaus encampment on September 18, 1827, two days before the promised deadline. The men were excited to see him, until they heard about the massacre at the Colorado River and learned that Smith had brought no supplies.

But the trappers at the camp had been busy: they had gathered a huge supply of furs, which would be valuable in obtaining more horses, rifles, and supplies. The party set off for Mission San José. There, Smith was escorted to Monterey—and promptly thrown in jail. He tried to explain to the authorities why he was back in California after agreeing to leave forever; again, the Spanish couldn't or wouldn't understand him. And again he was befriended by an American ship captain who, along with four other Americans, agreed to post a $30,000 bond for Smith's release.

Once more, Smith was free—this time, on two conditions. Firstly, he must sell his furs to the ship's captain at $2.50 a pound, a total of about $4,000. The price was low, but Smith had little choice. It would allow the captain to make a tidy profit on the furs in the East, which would partly repay his kindness. Secondly, Smith must leave

California, taking the way he had come. The authorities made it clear: Smith should never show his face there again. The Spanish would give him no third chance.

Smith sailed to San Francisco to rejoin his men. The sea was not his element—he was seasick during most of the voyage.

Smith broke his promise to the Spanish again. He took his men and their newly purchased horses and supplies back to the Stanislaus River, arriving there on January 1, 1828. This time he didn't head east over the mountains—it would have been too difficult and dangerous in winter. Instead, he traveled up the San Joaquin Valley and into the mountains of northern California.

Game was plentiful. The men had soon loaded their pack animals with more furs. One night, they trapped twenty beavers. "As I had but twenty-eight traps I considered it great trapping," Smith wrote in his journal. The trappers also encountered many bears. On one occasion, several bears attacked members of the party at once. Smith—a veteran of attack—dove into a stream to escape.

The party trapped their way northward, reaching the sea near present-day Crescent City, California, on June 8, and the Rogue River (Oregon) on June 27. On July 11, they traveled three miles up the Umpqua River. The trappers spent time trading with the local Umpqua (or Kelwatset) Indians for beaver skins, elk meat, and fish. On the morning of July 14, Smith and two men—John Turner and Richard Leland, the latter an Englishman who had joined the group in California—left in a canoe to do some scouting.

While they were gone, tragedy struck again. The Umpquas came into the camp. An incident over a stolen axe, or perhaps some argument over the trading, turned violent. The Indians stabbed or clubbed almost all of the trappers to death. Only a burly man named Arthur Black managed to escape, despite several stab wounds. For four days,

Black wandered through the woods, losing his clothing and knife to other Indians. He finally came across some friendly Indians who guided him to the Willamette Valley and from there to the Hudson's Bay outpost at Fort Vancouver. Black arrived at the British fur company's outpost on August 8.

Smith and the others had returned to camp unaware of the tragedy. The Umpquas fired on them, but they escaped, leaving all their furs and supplies behind, and made their way to the ocean. Near the Alsea River, they, too, were befriended by local Indians who guided them north. Amazingly, Smith and the others arrived at Fort Vancouver just two days after their wounded companion, Arthur Black.

In an unusual act of cooperation between fur trade rivals, the head of Hudson's Bay operations offered to help Smith and his fellow trappers. Usually, Dr. John McLoughlin jealously guarded his domain. Now he extended considerable courtesies to the unfortunate trappers in redressing the wrongs done them by the Umpquas. McLoughlin wanted peaceful relations with the Native Americans of the Northwest, and he wanted to stop the cycle of revenge immediately. The next incident could very well affect his own men.

Jed Smith and his three men joined Alexander McCleod (one of McLoughlin's agents), twenty-two Hudson's Bay men, and fourteen Indians on a trip up the Willamette. After weeks of coercion, threats, and some violence, the Umpquas agreed to retrieve as much of the stolen goods as possible. The trappers recovered hundreds of beaver pelts, twenty-two large and twenty small river otter skins, and five sea otter pelts along with several dozen horses and assorted rifles, traps, and other goods.

The party returned to the site of the ambush along the Umpqua River and spent a somber hour searching for their dead companions.

They located the bleached skeletons of eleven men. The other three were never found.

McLoughlin bought the recovered furs, though he reported (as any good trader would) that the furs were of poor quality. To partially repay McLoughlin for the company's kindness, Smith gave the British as much information as he could about the Sierra Nevada, northern California, and the Great Basin. Smith pocketed almost $2,400 from the sale of the furs, which allowed him and Arthur Black to trap streams of the Northwest all the way to the Canadian border before returning to the Rockies. At Flathead Lake (in present-day Montana), they met up with one of Smith's partners, David Jackson.

When they arrived at Pierre's Hole for the 1829 Rendezvous, the three partners paid off all of their debts to Ashley and walked away with a handsome profit. Smith reaped considerable financial success from his travels across the western lands. But the human toll was startling. On his two trips to California, spread over three years, he had taken thirty-three men—twenty-six were killed and two deserted.

Jed Smith and his partners continued to operate what had been William Ashley's company until the Rendezvous of 1830. By then, even the most optimistic trapper could see that the fur trade was in decline. Beaver populations were significantly reduced and demand was starting to wane. Competition was increasing. Anticipating a downturn, Smith, Sublette, and Jackson decided to sell out to a group of trappers that included Jim Bridger and others.

With $18 thousand in his pocket, Smith counted himself a relatively wealthy man. He took a few more exploring trips on the upper Missouri, then decided to retire to St. Louis. He was now able to help his family financially. He even bought himself a farm and two slaves.

As a man who had spent most of his life exploring on horseback or on foot, Jed Smith was not content to be a gentleman farmer. After a modest amount of pleading on the part of his friends, he agreed to accompany several experienced hands on a trading trip to Santa Fe. His old employer and partner, William Ashley, successfully petitioned Senator Thomas Hart Benton for a passport to make the trip.

The party headed south in the spring of 1831 with twenty-three wagons and eighty-five men—including two of Jed Smith's brothers and several famous mountain men and fur trappers. Crossing the barren lands of Comanche territory, somewhere between the Arkansas and Cimarron rivers, the travelers ran short of water. In late May 1831, Smith and the famous scout "Broken Hand" Fitzgerald went on ahead to scout for water, but Fitzgerald's horse went lame and he was forced to return to the wagon train. Jed Smith went on alone. He was never heard from again.

Eventually, the wagon train made it to Santa Fe, but found no news of Jedediah Smith. His body was never recovered. Later, a clue to Smith's fate turned up in Santa Fe. Mexican traders returning to the settlement after parleying with Comanches brought back Jed Smith's rifle and pistols. Their version of the death of the West's greatest explorer came from the Comanches. A hunting party of fifteen to twenty warriors had been waiting to ambush buffalo at a water hole when Smith unwittingly stumbled into their trap. According to the Comanches, Smith was killed at the water hole. As he fell, he shot and killed one of the Comanche chiefs. Jedediah Smith was only thirty-two years old.

Smith left behind an amazing list of accomplishments. Unfortunately, portions of his many journals were later lost in fires in Texas, Missouri, Iowa, and Illinois. Enough documents survived, though, including Smith's many letters to family and friends, to provide an accurate record of his travels and views.

Perhaps most important among the results of Smith's work was the encouragement he gave to settlers of the Oregon Territory. He wrote a letter to the War Department detailing British strength in the Northwest and discussing the opportunities for immigrants from the United States to settle in the new territories. He pointed out that wagons could easily cross the Rocky Mountains by going over South Pass. That route, along the Platte and Sweetwater rivers, was much easier than struggling along the Missouri River. To further entice immigrants, Jedediah Smith supplied maps; these were incorporated into other maps used by thousands of travelers.

When he was young, Jedediah Smith once wrote down his life's goals: "Becoming a first-rate hunter . . . making myself thoroughly acquainted with the Indians . . . tracing out the sources of the Columbia River . . . and . . . making the whole profitable to me." How rare a human being who so thoroughly accomplishes his goals, and more besides. ■

~ Across the Desert

The Patties

*M*ountain men led a dangerous life. They lived through bitter cold in the mountains, where snow could drift higher than a horse. Any Indians they met might turn out hostile; a mountain man had to be on constant alert. Other dangers abounded: of hunger and thirst, of disease or broken bones, of poisonous snakes or hordes of mosquitoes.

James Ohio Pattie, as experienced a trapper as ever was, once awoke in the night along the Gila River in present-day Arizona to find a mountain lion standing on a log just ten feet away. Pattie also had numerous encounters with bears and once reported seeing 220 grizzlies in one day along the Arkansas River. He probably exaggerated, but maybe not by much. Many other trappers reported seeing dozens of grizzlies at a time; many mountain men were attacked by bears and documented the incidents.

Bears and other wild animals were just one more hazard for those who spent time in the remote lands. Pattie estimated that of the 116 men who left Santa Fe to go trapping in 1826, only 16 were still alive the following year. James Pattie and his father, Sylvester, were nearly numbered among those casualties.

≈ ≈ ≈

The Patties came from Kentucky. James's father was born while his own father was off fighting Indians; Sylvester grew up no stranger to hard work and the outdoor life. During the War of 1812, Sylvester Pattie distinguished himself in battle against the British and their Indian allies.

James, Sylvester's oldest child, was eight years old when his father moved the family to southern Missouri. Sylvester Pattie planned to open a mill on the Gasconade River. When Sylvester's wife died from tuberculosis in 1823, he and James left the rest of the family with relatives in Kentucky. Father and son headed for the upper Missouri River to make their fortunes.

In St. Louis, the Patties fully outfitted themselves as fur trappers. They made their way upriver as far as Council Bluffs, where they stopped off to begin their new life. Green and inexperienced, though, they hadn't realized they would need a license to trap in Indian territory—a license they should have secured in St. Louis.

Undaunted, the Patties simply changed their plans and headed south. They joined a large trading caravan led by Sylvester Pratte. The two Kentuckians figured the caravan would escort them to Santa Fe in relative safety. From there, they could trap throughout the virtually unexplored southern Rockies. The caravan included many veterans of the War of 1812—experienced men who taught the Patties about trapping and dealing with various tribes.

Soon, a long relationship began between the Patties and Native Americans, much of it violent on both sides. Indian troubles commenced early in the trip. The travelers met with one Pawnee tribe in peace, but encountered hostile Pawnees farther south. Arikaras attacked one of their camps. Crows scalped two of the travelers. And Mescalero Apaches enacted a bloody scene during which another trader was killed.

Near where James Pattie reported seeing so many grizzly bears in a single day, a bear attacked a horse and proceeded to eat the stricken animal while it was still alive. James shot and wounded the grizzly; this only made it mad. Before it died, the bear charged into camp and tore one of the men to pieces. It was an eventful trip to Santa Fe.

James Pattie was fascinated with the Spanish lands, the people, and their customs. Both Patties began to learn the language. The governor gave them permission to trap beaver in Spanish territories.

James later explained his popularity in Santa Fe by telling this story of his heroism. Comanches had attacked several ranchos, killing the men and kidnapping five women. Pattie and a number of other trappers joined up with some Mexican soldiers to track down the Indians and rescue their captives. In James's version, three of the women and ten trappers were killed in the melee. James rescued the other two women—one of them the daughter of the ex-governor.

The story may or may not have been true. In recounting his adventures, James Pattie tended to embellish, exaggerate, and put himself into incidents that truly involved others. In any case, the local Mexican officials and residents took a liking to the Patties and were extremely hospitable to them.

Once the local authorities had sanctioned their trapping, the Patties enlisted twelve men and headed for the Gila River. They followed the Rio del Norte (Rio Grande) to the Santa Rita copper mines of present-day New Mexico. There, they hired two locals to guide them to the headwaters of the Gila (or "Helay," as James spelled it). The

TRAPPER GUARDING THE CAMP
ETCHING FROM *SCRIBNER'S MONTHLY*, MAY 1871

Patties suspected that rich beaver lands might lie along the Gila.

They were right. In the mountains of Arizona, the Gila's waters were cool and surrounded by forests. One of the Gila's tributaries—the Salt—supported especially abundant beaver populations. When the Patties arrived on October 6, they immediately set out traps.

Here, disagreements between Sylvester—the group's leader—and some of the men came to a head. Before the trapping expedition had set out, Sylvester drew up an agreement for all the men to sign. It listed explicit penalties for those who violated rules of conduct while in the wild. Anyone who disobeyed orders would be tried by a jury of fellow trappers. If found guilty, the offender would be fined fifty dollars, payable in furs. Anyone who deserted would be shot.

The men had all signed, but when they reached their first camp, some began to balk at Sylvester's rules and ignore his orders. Seven of the trappers left abruptly. The others were divided over what to do. In the end, the rules of agreement broke down and the rebel trappers were allowed to go.

It later turned out that the seven men, instead of turning back, had pushed onward to the headwaters of the Gila. The waters were filled with beaver and the deserters trapped every animal they could find. When Sylvester and his remaining men arrived, they found only carcasses—not a single live beaver. Hungry and tired, the party pressed on to the San Francisco River near present-day Clifton. There they found virgin beaver waters. In the first night, they trapped thirty-seven beavers. Even better, they found plenty of game to eat.

After a while, the men cached their growing collection of pelts and headed down the Gila River. One day they saw four of their former companions—assumed to have left those parts long before—approaching them through the woods. The men asked sheepishly to rejoin the Patties. Their group, they explained, had been attacked by

Indians. One man was killed and another badly wounded. The Indians stole all their horses. The survivors had wandered the mountains on foot for five days before finding the Patties. A day later, the wounded trapper arrived at the camp too.

Sylvester and James wanted to attack the Indians and recover the horses and furs, but the others had little stomach for contact with a hostile tribe. Neither did the survivors of the attack. So, showing generosity and restraint despite the men's desertion, as well as a frontier sense of decency, Sylvester allowed the survivors of the attack to leave. He outfitted them, gave them food, and let them return to the Santa Rita mines.

One chapter remained in the incident with the Indians. When the Patties reached the site of the splinter group's camp, they found the remains of the man who had been killed. His body had been cut into quarters "after the fashion of the butchers," James observed. The Indians had severed the man's head from his body and had used it for arrow target practice. The Indians were long gone, and the men buried the remains of the dead trapper.

The event further shaped James Pattie's views on Native Americans. Justifiably or not, Pattie seldom trusted an Indian tribe. He became an avowed Indian hater. Over the years, he witnessed and described many acts of savagery on the part of Indians—and he inflicted his own share of atrocities on them. It is difficult to separate truth from exaggeration in his tales. Enough other evidence exists to conclude that some southwestern tribes did use torture as a weapon against the encroaching whites. But Pattie may have embellished his descriptions of mutilation and torture to justify similar acts on his part.

After burying the dead trapper, Sylvester Pattie and his men spent two weeks wandering across the high desert of the Gila drainage.

~ The Patties' first fur-trapping expedition.

Finally, they found beaver-rich waters again. They trapped for several days and considered returning home. After all, despite the furs lost by the rebel trappers, they had done quite well.

Unfortunately, another group of Indians came upon the party in the early morning hours and drove off their horses. The men now had a good quantity of pelts and no way to transport them back. Again caching their furs, the travelers made the slow walk from the Gila River back to the Santa Rita mines in New Mexico. The trip was hot, miserable, and hundreds of miles long. Food was scarce. One day, the seven travelers shared a raven for breakfast and a turkey buzzard for dinner. They finally made it back to the mines.

James later returned to Santa Fe and outfitted another trip to the Gila to recover the cached furs. They were too late; someone had discovered their hiding places and taken all the furs.

Life at the Santa Rita copper mines was too tranquil for the Patties, though Apaches attacked periodically. But the father and son had come to the Southwest to make their fortunes and so far they had little to show for their efforts. Then an opportunity arose. The owner of the mines, tired of the regular Apache attacks, decided to lease his operation. For a thousand dollars a year, several Americans took over the running of the mine; Sylvester Pattie was named manager.

Here was a chance, Sylvester felt, to make a considerable amount of money. He urged James to join the operation, but the younger man still had wandering in his blood. While his father remained at Santa Rita, James joined another trapping party headed for Gila country.

James left his father on January 2, 1826, and traveled to the Gila River. At the junction of the Gila and Salt rivers, the party prepared to spend the night in a Papago (Tohono O'odham) village, where they had found a warm reception. But James had misgivings. He still trusted Indians only so far. He and another trapper set up camp outside the village.

James's distrust served him well that night. About midnight, the Indians attacked and killed all the trappers except one—Miguel Robidoux. Robidoux stumbled around in the darkness and managed to escape. Eventually, he found James and his companion and the three fled. As luck would have it, another trapping party was in the vicinity, led by well-known trapper/trader Ewing Young. Young found the three men, heard their story, and immediately planned a counterattack on the village.

Their revenge was swift. They killed several Indians, burned the village, and recovered the bodies of the unfortunate trappers. "A sight more horrible I have never seen," wrote James. "They were literally cut to pieces and fragments of their bodies scattered in every direction." Again, James Pattie had to bury the body parts of his traveling companions.

Rather than risk the trip back to Santa Rita, Pattie and the others elected to join Ewing and the rest of his men, an experienced band of trappers that included Ceran St. Vrain and "Old Bill" Williams. Trapping up the Salt and Verde rivers, the party split, then rejoined. They made their way from one beaver stream to the next.

The group soon encountered Yumans and Mojaves, the latter either just before or just after a visit from the trapper and explorer Jedediah Smith. The Mojaves were far from cordial. One of the chiefs speared a horse, and four of Ewing's men shot him dead in his tracks. Emotions boiled over. Just before dawn, the Mojaves attacked. The trappers killed sixteen warriors in the battle.

The white men knew they had to get out of Mojave territory as fast as possible. Young and his party retreated upriver, keeping on the move for four days. Finally, thinking they were well out of harm's way, the men made camp and fell fast asleep—without a guard.

It was a mistake. The Mojaves, determined to seek revenge, had dogged the trappers upriver. They had waited for a vulnerable moment such as this. After dark, the Indians showered arrows—some of them possibly tipped with poison—onto the sleeping trappers. Two men were killed outright and another two wounded. The man sleeping beside James was killed. Pattie leaped to his feet and ran for cover, just barely escaping arrows that pinned his blanket to the ground.

The cycle of revenge continued. In their turn, the trappers followed the Mojaves. They caught up with a small band that had stopped to eat part of a horse beneath a stand of cottonwoods. The whites killed all the Indians and, in a warning to the others, suspended the dead bodies from the cottonwoods.

From that day on, the trappers were wary. They never worked without setting guards. But even this precaution wasn't foolproof. One day, James went looking for three trappers missing from the party. At midday, he came across a sickening sight. In an arroyo, a small group of Indians sat roasting the cut-up bodies of the missing men over a fire. The Indians fled and James once again had to bury dismembered bodies.

Ewing Young's party eventually explored thousands of miles of territory. They went up the Colorado River and in 1826 were the first whites to see the Grand Canyon. From there, they wandered over three hundred miles of desolate country, plagued by hunger and huge snow drifts in the mountains.

No one knows exactly where Young, Pattie, and the others traveled in their search for beaver. The accounts James Pattie left behind are full of errors and vague descriptions. The group does seem to have crossed the Rockies on a snowy trail packed down by the passage of many buffalo. According to James Pattie, the party trapped all the way up to the Yellowstone River. It is unlikely that they explored so far north; they may have made it as far as the South Platte River.

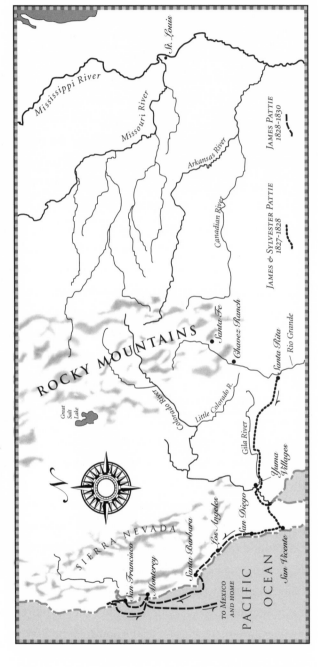

The Patties' journey west from the Santa Rita Copper Mines.

One event clearly did take place: another band of Indians caught up with the trappers—maybe Blackfeet and maybe on the upper Arkansas—and killed four of them. The Blackfeet lost sixteen of their own men in the scuffle. The survivors, their animals loaded with beaver pelts, finally made it back. Young had lost one-third of his men; he brought back $20 thousand worth of beaver skins. In Santa Fe, a new governor greeted him—one who refused to acknowledge Young's license to trap in Spanish territory. He promptly seized the party's furs. After all their trials, the Americans were left with nothing.

While his son was off risking life and limb, Sylvester Pattie had made a success of his copper mine. He was close to making the fortune he had long sought. Again, he urged his son to join him; but James wasn't the kind to stay put. He led a few trips to Santa Fe, bringing back supplies for the mine, but then he got the itchy foot and off he went.

In an encounter with a grizzly bear, James fell and cracked his jaw. When it had healed, he joined fifteen other Americans on a trapping expedition up a tributary of the Rio Grande. Their path took them through the heart of Mescalero Apache country. The Apaches attacked, and in the brief battle, James got an arrow in the hip and another in the chest. The trappers drove off the Apaches and soon took their revenge. According to James, the white men killed several Apaches; and as a warning to the rest, they cut off the heads of the dead.

Tough as a cob, James survived. But now his wanderlust waned. He decided to do as his father wished: they would leave New Mexico together as wealthy men. James knew that he had dodged the bullet, the arrow, and the bear paw too many times. Just as the father and son prepared to go back to Kentucky to rejoin their family, disaster struck. Sylvester had entrusted a clerk at the mine with $30 thousand

—the Patties' nest egg. The man saddled a horse one night and took off for Mexico. The Patties saw neither clerk nor money again.

Nearly broke, the Patties were forced to return to fur trapping. They obtained a new license to hunt in the Colorado-Gila area and signed on more than two dozen men. Again, Sylvester had made the men sign an agreement of conduct, and again, he faced a mutiny: twenty of the men left. Sylvester finally learned that trappers and mountain men were an independent lot, answering to few others. Rules were not for them. "Free trappers," or those who thought themselves such, played by their own notions.

The remaining eight men decided to go on, but they soon ran into trouble. As the party slept in their camp along the Colorado River one night, Yuman Indians stole their horses. The trappers found themselves stranded in a hot, desolate country populated by hostile Indians, with a big pile of furs and supplies.

Never completely at a loss, the men carved two canoes from cottonwood trees. They loaded their furs and paddled down the lower Colorado, eventually reaching the mouth of the river at the Gulf of California. Despite their hopes that the Colorado would take them west to present-day California, they were still far from their goal. In the delta region of the lower river, they did find rich beaver grounds, where they trapped thirty to sixty beavers a night. They also had more skirmishes with hostile tribes.

Finally, eighty miles below the mouth of the Gila River, they encountered the powerful tidal bore of the ocean; they could paddle no farther. The downstream rush of the Colorado at their backs prevented them from turning around. Their only option was to strike out across desolate lands (later known as Baja California del Norte) toward the missions of southern California. They hid their large supply of furs near the river and set off to the west.

The party's water soon gave out. The men's tongues started to swell. They were crossing the most barren furnace in North America with almost no protection from the relentless sun. A water hole in the middle of nowhere probably saved their lives—but within a couple of days, they were dying of thirst again. Their lips turned black. Some of the men tried drinking their own urine. It didn't help. They staggered on across the desert, their eyes half-blinded by the brightness. One man attempted suicide; he was too weak to succeed.

After endless miles, the party climbed over the crest of yet another arroyo and beheld a beautiful sight: a stream running clear and slow. Incredulous, they were running to immerse themselves in the water when two Indians appeared—Christian converts from the Mission of Santa Catalina. James was absolutely certain that the stream and their rescuers were direct gifts from God. The Indians, in their turn, couldn't believe these men had even attempted to cross the desert of northern Baja California. The Patties and their comrades were the first to have done it.

When the trappers had quenched their thirst, the Indians guided them to the Mission. But James's moccasins had worn out and his feet were cut and infected. He had to wait by the river until the missionaries sent two more Indians to carry him. They arrived at the Mission on March 18, 1828.

Like Jedediah Smith, who had arrived unannounced and unwanted in California, the Patties and their party were considered spies. From Mission Santa Catalina, they were moved under armed guard to Mission San Sebastian and, eventually, to San Diego. There, they met the governor, José-Maria Echeandìa—the same man who had imprisoned Jedediah Smith earlier. Smith had twice tricked the governor, staying in California after he had promised to leave. Echeandìa was still seething about it, and the Patties' arrogant attitude didn't help. This time, the governor swore, he would have no mercy on illegal immigrants from the United States. He threw the Patties in jail and tore up their passports, calling them "worse than thieves and murderers."

For Sylvester Pattie, it was the beginning of the end. Weakened by the ordeal of crossing the desert and the weeks he spent in the Spanish jail, Sylvester died in prison in 1828. The rest of the party were more fortunate. The captain of a ship from New England persuaded the governor to let the men return to the Colorado River to retrieve the furs they had hidden. Undoubtedly, the captain and the governor both saw a handsome profit for themselves if James Pattie were ransomed for the furs.

The party returned to the hiding place but all they found were ruined pelts. Spring floods on the Colorado River had reached the hidden furs before the trappers did. Two of the men deserted, assuming—correctly—that they would be imprisoned again if they returned empty-handed. The other four returned to report the bad news.

James remained in jail until he was released because of a smallpox epidemic. His story is highly improbable, but a thread of truth runs through it. At the time, smallpox was slowly making its way through California. The governor had made several desperate requests for vaccine from Mexico City but had not received any. According to James, Sylvester had brought a small supply of vaccine with him, and James knew how to administer it. A chance conversation between one of the trappers and a guard brought the news to the governor, who demanded that James vaccinate the local residents. James refused to do it unless the governor gave him his freedom in exchange. According to James, the governor also promised money.

The whole of James Pattie's story is probably an exaggeration. Smallpox did break out in California. But James's claim that he vaccinated 22,000 people from San Diego to San Francisco is obviously far-fetched. But Pattie really was released from prison and he did receive written approval from the governor to travel in California. Some of his fellow trappers remained in California, married local women, and became Mexican citizens.

James, however, had no desire to stay, and he believed the governor had reneged on an agreement. Pattie worked on a coastal ship, dabbled in the sea otter fur trade, and finally made his way to Mexico City. There, he petitioned the government for the money he claimed was due him. According to Pattie, government officials agreed that his claim had merit, but since the government was broke, they awarded him nothing.

Dejected, James went to Vera Cruz and, with the last of his money, purchased passage on a ship bound for New Orleans. He intended to return to his family in Kentucky, but he ended up stranded in New Orleans, broke. Fortunately, he happened to meet one of Louisiana's senators, Josiah Johnston. The senator said he knew some of the Patties. He was going upriver on the steamship *Cora*, bound for Cincinnati, and he paid James's forty-dollar passage too.

Throughout the trip, Johnston sat and listened in amazement to Pattie's stories of his adventures in the Southwest. From that point, things happened quickly. Johnston gave James a letter of introduction to a friend, the popular writer Timothy Flint. Before long, James Pattie was dictating his memoirs to Flint. They were soon published as *The Personal Narrative of James O. Pattie, of Kentucky*. The book enjoyed immediate success and was widely read for decades. More importantly for James, the book provided him with enough money to make the forty-mile trip upriver to the family home. Some of his relatives still lived there, but his siblings had scattered long before.

His memoirs are a fascinating account of the adventures of

Sylvester and James Pattie, or others, or some combination of the two. The tale is short on dates and long on exaggeration. Apparently, however, Flint based at least part of the book on written journals that James had kept. Despite the lack of historical detail, the book's essential elements are true enough, and it is one of the few narratives "written" by a mountain man about what life was really like in those days.

As for James Ohio Pattie, his fate is something of a mystery. His relatives believed that he died in the snows of the Sierra Nevada in the winter of 1849–50 or the winter after that, on his way to the gold fields. If the story is true, his death was a logical sequel to his wild younger years. But James Pattie last appeared on the Kentucky tax rolls in the early 1830s. His relatives couldn't account for the fifteen years in between when he seems to have dropped out of existence.

Others suspect the veteran fur trapper may have died unglamorously in the 1833 cholera outbreak. There was no reliable sighting of James Pattie after 1833. The bodies of hundreds of cholera victims were buried quickly to prevent the spread of disease. No one kept a record of the dead, and even local residents couldn't say who all had gone. James Pattie might have been among them. ▪

CHAPTER NINE

⁓ Explorer by Sea

Charles Wilkes

*K*ing Kamehameha had authorized two hundred porters to carry the supplies and scientific instruments for the party of sixteen Americans. Lieutenant Charles Wilkes of the United States Navy signaled to his men. In single file they went, wading through the lush undergrowth. It was slow going through the forest. Day after day, the group pressed onward, gradually gaining elevation. They heard occasional sounds from above. But not until the ninth day did they reach the summit of Mauna Loa and witness the spectacle of steam and molten lava.

The scientists were ecstatic. Wilkes himself admitted that he had felt excited when he peered into the crater of the living, smoking volcano. "The color of its burning contents was that of a cherry-red or deep crimson. . . . The whole surface was in the most violent agitation."

Charles Wilkes, leader of the United States Exploring Expedition, was conducting a six-week study of Mauna Loa and the other Hawaiian volcanoes. But even as he stood atop this mountain in a tropical paradise, his eyes wandered to the eastern horizon. Soon, they would need to leave, in order to undertake the next and most important segment of their journey: the exploration of the Oregon Territory—not from the land, but from the Pacific Ocean.

～ ～ ～

Wilkes was born on April 3, 1798, in New York City, the son of a well-to-do businessman. His father had hoped that young Charles would enter the banking profession. Charles had other ideas. He had always loved the sea. At age seventeen, he signed on as a cabin boy on a sailing ship bound for France. So began a long and memorable career as a sailor.

When he was twenty, Wilkes was made a midshipman aboard an American man-of-war. He won acclaim as a navigator and chart maker. His curiosity extended to various scientific fields. Wilkes's big opportunity came in 1836, and, like many things that happened in his life, it brought controversy with it. In this instance, he was granted an appointment many others had coveted.

On May 18, 1836, Congress authorized expenditures for a great expedition—the United States Exploring Expedition—that would survey the southern oceans and chart the potential for harvesting whales and seals. As plans for the expedition developed, it grew to include scientists and artists who would join the naval crew and collect scientific samples.

The expedition's goals also expanded to include accurate surveys of many lands—some uncharted and others little visited. One additional objective quickly became a major component of the trip: an accurate survey of the lands, bays, and coastline of the territory between San Francisco and Vancouver Island. In the end, the flotilla

CHARLES WILKES

U.S. Naval Academy Museum

was to include six ships, making it the largest American naval excursion ever undertaken.

Competition for the command of the expedition was keen. Of the forty lieutenants in the Navy at that time, thirty-eight had performed more sea duty than Charles Wilkes. Yet, Wilkes received the appointment, partly because he had scientific and surveying experience. Whether political pressure in some way helped Wilkes isn't known. The controversy surrounding the appointment, however, affected Wilkes throughout his career.

The flotilla left Hampton Road, Virginia, on August 18, 1838. The six ships that set sail were the *Vincennes*, a sloop-of-war and Wilkes's flagship; the *Peacock*, another sloop; the schooners *Sea Gull* and *Flying Fish*; the brig *Porpoise*; and the navy's first supply ship, the *Relief*.

As the expedition headed toward the Madeira Islands, their first stop, Wilkes discovered that the *Relief* moved too slowly. It held the other ships back, and would make a long voyage even longer. Eventually, the crew transferred the supplies to the other ships and sent the *Relief* home.

The remaining ships headed on to Rio de Janeiro. There, the scientists went ashore to collect specimens of plants and animals, while Wilkes and some of his men explored the surrounding land. They made similar stops all down the eastern coast of South America, arriving at Tierra del Fuego, the continent's southern tip, on January 30, 1839.

Charles Wilkes's upbringing had not prepared him to appreciate the native peoples of other lands—or Native Americans for that matter. He was not shy about giving his opinion of the Tierra del Fuegans: "They are not more than five feet high, of a light coffee color, which is much concealed by smut and dirt, which they mark vertically with charcoal. . . . It is impossible to fancy any thing in human nature more filthy. They are an ill-shappen and ugly race."

The southern hemisphere's summer was far from mild in this remote area. Despite the cold, Wilkes prepared to undertake a unique exploration. For centuries, the Antarctic region had been known to exist. Yet, on charts, it appeared vague. Was the South Pole simply an ice-covered sea? Did solid land lie there? If so, was the land connected to one of the continents? Captain Cook had traveled south into that brutal climate, but not far enough to answer these questions. Wilkes's men hoped to break the Englishman's record and venture even closer to the Pole.

Anxious to press on with the mission, Wilkes headed south toward Palmer's Land, Antarctica aboard the *Porpoise*, with the *Sea Gull* sailing alongside. The second in command, William Hudson, took the *Peacock* and *Flying Fish* to explore toward the southwest. The first week of March had arrived: the wind howled, sleet and snow pelted the men's faces, and thirty-two-foot-high waves pummeled the *Porpoise* and the *Sea Gull*. Huge icebergs drifted nearby. Though the two sailing ships had copper-sheathed hulls, neither would have survived a collision with an iceberg.

On March 3, the *Porpoise* sighted Palmer's Land. Though he was so close, Wilkes surrendered to bad weather and turned the ships back to Tierra del Fuego. The *Peacock* didn't fare any better. A man fell from the icy main mast and was lost overboard. The *Flying Fish* traveled farther west, found better weather, and eventually sighted what appeared to be land. Even their trip was a frightening experience. Eventually, all four ships abandoned the Antarctic exploration. They rejoined the *Vincennes* and headed up the west coast of South America.

The journey northward was worse. Rounding the tip of South America in a storm, the *Sea Gull* disappeared with all hands on board. The remaining four ships continued up the Chilean coast to Peru,

USS VINCENNES

Courtesy, Peabody Essex Museum, Salem, MA

stopping in Lima and Callao. Wilkes took copious notes about the people, their cities, and their customs. He was especially interested in the Peruvians.

Eight months into the trip, the sailors' morale was sinking. Most of the crew despised Lieutenant Wilkes; behind his back, they called him "the Stormy Petrel." Wilkes, in turn, suspected his officers of plotting against him. He moved crews from ship to ship, demoted officers regularly, and even dismissed an entire boatload of sailors, sending them ashore in Peru. Even more troubling to the officers and crew was Wilkes's appearance on deck one day, dressed in a naval captain's uniform—he had apparently promoted himself while at sea.

Whatever his personal shortcomings, Wilkes continued to distinguish himself as a navigator, chart maker, and dynamic leader. When the four ships headed west from Callao on July 13, 1839, Wilkes devised a plan to increase the expedition's surveying productivity. As they reached each island group, Wilkes divided the area into segments and assigned each ship and its launches a segment. The explorers were thus able to chart an enormous area of the South and Central Pacific. In all, they mapped 280 islands, including those in the Tonga, Samoa, Gilbert (now Kiribati), Ellice (now Tuvalu), Society (including Tahiti), Union (now Tokelau), Marquesas, Marshall, Fiji, and Phoenix island groups, and many others.

Despite Charles Wilkes's avid interest in science, he hated the "scientifics"—his name for the nine scientists and artists on the expedition. Most of the nine were either well-known before they joined the expedition or would become so in the years after it ended. The "scientifics" included James Dana, a geologist who was also a famous zoologist; Titian Peale, an artist, naturalist, and expert marksman (he had been a member of Stephen Long's expedition to the Great Plains almost twenty years before); Joseph Drayton and Andrew Agate, renowned artists—they produced outstanding drawings of fish, mammals, and scenery on the trip; and Charles Pickering, a medical doctor and zoologist who served as the expedition's ethnologist, studying the native peoples and their customs.

Wilkes openly despised the civilians, and they hated him back. The lieutenant felt they failed to appreciate his scientific opinions; he was probably envious of their extensive academic backgrounds. Even the officers and crew grew weary of ferrying the scientists ashore and catering to their huge collection of specimens. The sailors called the civilians "bug catchers" or "clam diggers." Wilkes finally forbade the scientists to study animals below decks because of the noxious smells of their chemicals. In their turn, the scientists complained that too much time was spent surveying and not enough collecting.

If the petty bickering of people confined to close quarters for long periods of time was one thing, the physical dangers of exploring the

South Sea Islands was another. Shore parties came under attack on several occasions. In the Fijis, after an otherwise peaceful shore leave of a month, two of the sailors were killed. One of them was Wilkes's nephew. The captain's response was swift and violent: he sent men ashore to burn two villages. Fifty-six Fijians died. Titian Peale shot two Fijians from a distance of 215 yards.

Another time, when a party put ashore to fill water barrels, a sailor was killed. Several such incidents occurred; sometimes the sailors initiated the violence. When they landed on an island, the explorers didn't know whether they would be attacked or showered with gifts. Some native people welcomed them heartily; in contrast, they had heard that many Fiji Island natives were cannibals.

In late 1839, the four ships reached Australia. Temporarily leaving the "scientifics" behind, Wilkes took his ships back to Antarctica for another attempt at exploration. This time, the sailors spotted land. They even dredged up rocks from 360 fathoms along the coast. Then ice shattered the *Peacock*'s rudder. The ship and its crew almost went down in the freezing water; by great luck, the vessel ricocheted off an ice cliff and careened into open water. There, the ship's carpenters were able to build and mount a new rudder.

Aboard the *Vincennes*, Wilkes explored the new land as thoroughly as time allowed, charting over 1500 miles of coastline. He was the first person to prove that Antarctica was a separate continent. On February 21, 1840, the ships left Antarctica for Australia. Wilkes retrieved the "scientifics" and headed for Hawaii, then known as the Sandwich Islands, stopping at several other islands en route. The expedition's three months in Hawaii included extensive studies of volcanoes and rich communities of plants and birds. But problems continued to plague Wilkes's command.

When the ships arrived in Hawaii in September of 1840, the men were sick and demoralized; they cared little about further exploring. Already a year behind schedule, the journey had become known as the "everlasting expedition." The long shore leave in a tropical paradise was tranquil, and the enlistments of fifty men had expired. The men elected to stay in Hawaii. Wilkes offered an even longer shore leave; he promised more pay; he warned the sailors that they would be stranded for a long time before ever reaching home; all to no avail. Working under the command of the Stormy Petrel could not compare with life in paradise. Some of Wilkes's best sailors left him; he had to hire Hawaiians to fill out his crews.

And the most important segment of the expedition still lay ahead. Wilkes knew that his surveys of the Oregon Territory could prove critical in his country's acquisition of new land, and in its general success as a nation. Besides, Wilkes's officers and men had now been away from the North American continent for almost two years. He had to hurry.

The *Vincennes* and the *Porpoise* left Hawaii on April 5, 1841, sailing directly for the mouth of the Columbia River. Lieutenant Hudson again took the *Peacock* and the *Flying Fish*, sailing eastward to explore more islands and, eventually, northward to rendezvous with the others.

Wilkes arrived at the mouth of the Columbia in April of 1841. His first view of the river's treacherous bar alarmed him: "Mere description can give little idea of the terrors of the bar of the Columbia: all who have seen it have spoken of the wilderness of the scene, and the incessant roar of the waters, representing it as one of the most fearful sights that can possibly meet the eye of the sailor."

Despite his sailing skills, or perhaps because of them, and even with an experienced pilot on board, Wilkes decided not to chance a landing. Instead, he headed north to the Strait of Juan de Fuca and into Puget Sound. He discovered the sound with relief and delight:

he had found the key to trade with the countries of the Pacific—it was this inland waterway, not the Columbia River as so many had assumed.

The potential value to the United States of Puget Sound truly impressed Wilkes: "Nothing can exceed the beauty of these waters, and their safety: not a shoal exists within the Straits of Juan de Fuca, Admiralty Inlet, Puget Sound or Hood's Canal, that can in any way interrupt their navigation by a seventy-four gun ship. I venture nothing in saying, there is no country in the world that assesses waters equal to these."

Wilkes knew what had to be done: his country must acquire Puget Sound in a land settlement with the British, at any cost. At the time of his visit, two treaties were in force designating joint occupancy of the territory. Wilkes's surveys would be critical to any decisions the United States might make concerning these northwestern lands.

The Hudson's Bay Company had an outpost at Nisqually, and the British fur traders treated Wilkes's crew as their guests. They gave the captain presents of wooden masks carved by local Native Americans.

Using George Vancouver's decades-old charts, Wilkes worked to improve the maps and correct the errors. From Nisqually, he sent out parties to collect, explore, measure, and map. James Dana was fascinated by the geology of the area. He found several large peaks that he suspected were recent volcanoes. One group of men, led by Lieutenant Robert Johnson, crossed the Cascades and explored the interior of what is now western Washington. Charles Pickering, the ethnologist, accompanied them and made careful notes on the tribes the party encountered. Dr. Pickering noted that the locals farmed and fished for salmon; some tribes constructed log cabins, others lived in tepees like those of the Plains Indians.

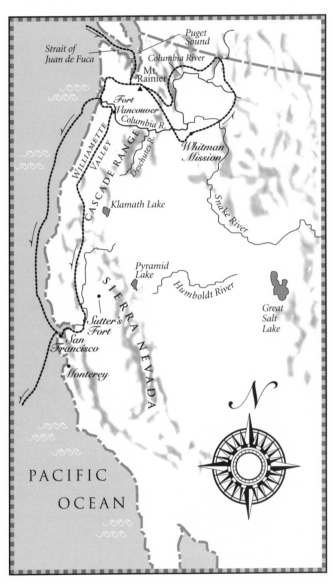

~ WILKES'S EXPLORATION OF THE PACIFIC
NORTHWEST AND PACIFIC COAST.

When the expedition finally left Nisqually, they returned to the mouth of the Columbia, expecting to find Hudson there. His ships were nowhere in sight. Rather than wait, Wilkes elected to go upriver to visit Fort Vancouver, another Hudson's Bay trading post in the command of Dr. John McLoughlin. From there, Wilkes sent out more parties, directing them to explore the Columbia Basin all the way to its junction with the Snake River.

What most impressed Wilkes in the northwestern territories was the settlement already taking place. Settlers had cultivated some nine square miles of farmland. The Cowlitz Farm alone supplied the Russians in Alaska with fifteen thousand bushels of grain, as well as butter and cheese. The area's American settlers asked Wilkes to help them establish an American-style government in the Oregon Territory. But a strong British presence led by McLoughlin asserted its right to govern. Clearly, a higher level of government would have to determine the status of the lands that would become British Columbia, Washington, Oregon, and Idaho. Charles Wilkes did make strong recommendations to his government. He predicted that California and the Oregon Territory would "control the destinies of the Pacific," especially through Puget Sound and San Francisco Bay.

Wilkes had left a lookout at the mouth of the Columbia to wait for Hudson's two ships. On July 17, 1841, they arrived, and Lieutenant Hudson decided to traverse the treacherous bar. Almost immediately, he knew he had made a mistake. The *Peacock* went aground in the middle of the bar and quickly took on water. The men scrambled into launches or jumped into the strong current. Local Chinook Indians came to the rescue and all hands were saved. But the ship was lost, along with most of the insect specimens and many of the scientists' Hawaiian collections.

John McLoughlin stepped in to help. He arranged for Wilkes to buy another ship and resupplied the expedition at a very low price. McLoughlin may have feared the impact so many Americans might have if the *Peacock*'s sailors had been discharged there. But his kindness came from a humanitarian impulse. Years before, he had helped trapper/explorer Jedediah Smith and his party when they came to the fort. In appreciation of McLoughlin's generosity, Lieutenant Hudson sent forty sailors to help the settlers harvest their crops.

From Fort Vancouver, Wilkes sent a party under Lieutenant George Emmon on a major journey up the Willamette Valley and across the mountains to the Sacramento River. The group encountered hostile Indian tribes and weathered a series of incidents before arriving at Sutter's Fort, near Sacramento. Surveying as they went, they stopped at the Mission San Jose before reaching Yerba Buena, soon to be known as San Francisco.

Wilkes, meanwhile, slowly worked his way down the coast of Oregon and northern California. He constructed such accurate maps of the area that the Secretary of the Navy later felt this single accomplishment justified the cost of the entire expedition. Wilkes sent James Dana ashore to study the geology of the region. At Saddle Mountain, south of present-day Astoria, Oregon, Dana discovered a rich deposit of fossil mollusks; he brought many of them back to the *Vincennes*. All the "scientifics" were excited about the opportunities for collecting.

Eventually, the ships reunited at San Francisco. The small flotilla returned to Hawaii to drop off the Hawaiian sailors, then sailed for the Philippines, Mindoro Straits, and the Sulu Sea, all of which they charted carefully. On shore leave in Singapore, Wilkes sold the *Flying Fish* to a local yachtsman. The ship was no longer seaworthy, but was apparently serviceable enough for the opium trade. It smuggled opium in and out of China for some time.

Rounding the Cape of Good Hope, the remaining ships headed

for home. Wilkes sent Hudson and the *Porpoise* to Rio de Janeiro for a final series of botanical collections, while the *Vincennes* sailed directly to the United States. The ship arrived at Sandy Hook, New Jersey, on June 10, 1842. The men had been gone for almost four years and had traveled 87,780 nautical miles under sail. Only two of the original ships made it home, along with half the original crew. The rest had left at various ports of call or died.

The United States Exploring Expedition had accomplished a monumental amount of exploration and discovery. Only as exceptional a seaman and as focused an individual as Charles Wilkes could have completed the objectives. Yet, few people, even in Congress, appreciated the implications of the trip. Charles Wilkes's abrasive personality robbed him of some of the consideration his achievements deserved. He was ultimately brought up before a court martial. Crewmen and officers called him a "monster." One lieutenant went so far as to say, "Wilkes merits hanging, only that he deserved impaling, long, long, ago." Wilkes ultimately received a mild reprimand. The Navy decided that the captain's accomplishments far outweighed his personality failures.

During the Civil War, Wilkes was again reprimanded for forcibly abducting two Confederate representatives off the British mail steamer *Trent*—an act that almost brought England into the war. Even then, Wilkes's minor reputation as a great explorer remained intact.

Personal weaknesses aside, Wilkes also suffered from an apathetic Congress and public. People found the flamboyant John C. Frémont, who was conducting a series of popular land expeditions at the time, more exciting.

Wilkes published his *Narrative of the U.S. Exploring Expedition During the Years 1838, 1839, 1840, 1841, 1842* in five volumes and two atlases of maps. The books included numerous drawings by Wilkes and the ships' artists. Wilkes had surveyed 1,500 miles of the coast of Antarctica, 800 miles of the Oregon Territory coastline, and 100 miles of the Columbia River. His maps of 280 islands of the South and Central Pacific were so accurate that the U.S. Navy and Marine Corps used them during World War II a hundred years later.

The expedition made unprecedented gains in scientific knowledge. Its members had gathered over 160,000 specimens of plants and animals including 4,000 zoological specimens representing 2,000 new species. Birds accounted for over 2,000 specimens and 500 species. Though some of the Hawaiian collections were lost in the wreck of the *Peacock*, a dozen specimens survived of the now-extinct honeyeater—the *o'o*, a bird that supplied the yellow feathers for Hawaiian ceremonial feather robes.

The ships brought back over 50,000 plants of 10,000 species, including a Hawaiian plant that was later named *Wilkesia* after the expedition's leader. Wilkes had returned with a huge number of live plant specimens: these formed the basis for establishing the Washington Botanical Gardens.

Add to this the thousands of native artifacts—weapons, clothing, masks, bowls—along with gems, coral, and other geological treasures: the total material would overwhelm any museum. That is exactly what happened. The country wasn't prepared to handle what Wilkes and his "scientifics" brought back. Many of the samples wandered in limbo until the National Institute for the Promotion of Science stored and displayed them in the New Patent Office Building in Washington, D.C.

Finally, in 1857, the new Smithsonian Institution took over the material. Charles Wilkes's specimens served as the founding collection of what would become one of the world's greatest museums (eventually several musuems). The Smithsonian spent decades analyzing Wilkes's material; some, such as the fishes, were never completely catalogued. The rest appeared in twenty-three volumes, covering geology, zoology, botany, coral reefs, ethnology, and meteorology. Describing new species and genera from the collection took well into the 1920s.

Still, the fame and promotion that Charles Wilkes sought evaded him. Outside scientific circles, few appreciated his enormous achievements. Congress only printed one hundred copies of his *Narrative*. Wilkes had to print the rest privately, just as Stephen Long had done with his underrated report over two decades earlier. Wilkes's report did convince President Polk that the United States should acquire the Pacific Northwest—at least the area between the Columbia River and Puget Sound.

The lack of notice was a bitter pill for Wilkes to swallow. Until his death in 1877, he worked on his memoirs and responded to attacks from Senator Thomas Hart Benton and others who claimed that some of his charts were flawed. They weren't. Many of the attacks came from the supporters of John C. Frémont. Benton was Frémont's father-in-law, and the senator used his considerable influence to discredit Frémont's competitors.

The acclaim that Charles Wilkes wished for came too late for him. His memoirs were finally published in 1978, over a hundred years after his death. The British appreciated Wilkes's work, and presented him with the Royal Geographical Society's prestigious Founders Medal. And at the end of his career, a certain degree of honor did come his way. Charles Wilkes was promoted to the rank of Rear Admiral. From his beginnings—the seventeen-year-old who disobeyed his father's wishes and ran off to sea as a cabin boy—Wilkes had come a long way. ■

CHAPTER TEN

~ The Trail to California

John C. Frémont

*J*ohn Frémont, his cartographer Charles Preuss, and five other men had spent the last two months in close company with many others on a great adventure to the Rocky Mountains. Now, Frémont's small party had separated from the rest to undertake an unusual journey back to the East.

Frémont had decided that on the return trip, he would run the rapids of the Platte River in a specially made rubber boat. Their horses had carried this collapsible boat all the way from Missouri to the Wind River Range in the Rocky Mountains. Now they would finally have a chance to use it. The craft was ready, fully loaded with scientific instruments, personal baggage, and food for a dozen days. The men pushed off from the shore and quickly joined the downstream flow of the Platte River.

People had traveled alongside much of the Platte River for decades, but the course of the river itself—its rapids and canyons—was less known. Each canyon seemed to take the men through a deep tunnel, littered with fragments of rock that had fallen from the heights of the sheer cliffs.

The crew conquered three series of rapids, one after another, before the canyon opened into a calm, flat region. Frémont waved the paddlers toward shore, where they ate a leisurely breakfast. Maybe the river would give them a pleasant diversion from days on horseback, the men thought. After all, traveling downstream wasn't too strenuous.

An hour later, the men pushed off again. The current immediately carried them into another deep canyon. Jagged rocks and swirling water filled the narrow chasm. The steep cliffs came right to the water's edge; there was no way to portage around the rapids. Charles Preuss waded ashore with their prized chronometer and tried to inch his way along the rocks to protect the valuable instrument. Eventually, the walls of another sheer canyon blocked his path and he had to jump aboard the rubber boat again.

The going got worse. It was impossible to turn back or to make progress forward. Frémont later wrote, "Our position was rather a bad one . . . before us the cataract was a sheet of foam . . . the roar of water was deafening." An unseen wave pulled a pair of saddlebags and a sextant from the boat. Frémont lurched forward and grabbed the sextant, but the bags and their contents disappeared overboard.

To continue seemed too dangerous, so three men stood on a tiny piece of shore and tried to lower the boat through the rapids using a fifty-foot length of rope. The current was much too powerful. The force of the rushing water pulled the rope from the hands of two of the men and jerked the third man into the swirling rapids. Basil Lajennesse looked like a tiny piece of debris in the foaming water. His head bobbed to the surface from time to time, then disappeared again. In an eddy downstream, Frémont and the others finally managed to rescue the soaked man, but it was a close call. The other two men scrambled aboard and the current again swept the vessel into the rapids. At this point, three of the men confessed that they could not swim.

By now, the adrenaline was flowing. Frémont's heart pounded. Around every bend lurked a new danger, a new challenge. To banish their fear, the men started singing—shouting the words to an old Canadian boat song at the top of their lungs. The river wasn't impressed. Swept along at high speed, the rubber vessel struck a hidden rock and flipped upside down, scattering men and supplies into the water.

Frémont feared for the three men who couldn't swim, but he was in no position to do much about it. He fought to keep his own head above water as he was swept downstream past jagged rocks. Luckily, the river dumped him in a quiet eddy and he managed to scramble atop a pile of rocks.

Twenty yards below him, Charles Preuss reached shore on the opposite bank. The waves cast the rubber boat ashore, upside down. The men who could swim reached those who couldn't in time, but the contents of the boat were scattered hundreds of yards downstream. Valuable instruments, still in their cases, bobbed in the water, then disappeared. The crew lost their sextant, a large telescope, two compasses, most of their clothing and food, and a journal containing valuable data on climate and map positions.

John Frémont stood on shore and looked at the debris scattered about, the soaked and exhausted men, and the overturned craft. He knew the disaster was his fault: he had been headstrong and adventuresome.

John C. Frémont was like that; he took ill-advised risks. He was also a skilled surveyor, a man who endured hardships along with his companions, and an explorer who became known as "the Pathfinder."

Two John Frémonts really coexisted within the one. The first was the public image: a bearded Frémont holding an American flag atop a Rocky Mountain peak or a Frémont on horseback, leading a rag-tag band of men into California during the Mexican War. The second Frémont was somewhat less appealing: he was the man who took full advantage of political connections and life's opportunities to maximize the effect of the first Frémont.

The truth is probably somewhere between those extremes. He was astute, he was flamboyant, and he was talented. Frémont did not discover as much new territory as some of his exploring predecessors; but he was the first to accurately map much of the West, covering more territory in western North America than any person of his day.

Frémont's young life was steeped in scandal. His mother left her husband to run off with Charles Fremon, a French dancing master. Their illegitimate son, John Charles, was born in 1813. Early in life, John added a "t" to his name, as well as an accent on the "e." No one ever knew why.

Frémont's mother came from a prominent Virginia family, but because of the scandal, she and her sons were destitute after Charles Fremon died. Despite their poverty, John entered the College of Charleston when he was sixteen. Frémont was bright, but he was expelled from school three months before his graduation for "incorrigible negligence." Five years later, Frémont petitioned the Board of Trustees and they awarded him a Bachelor of Arts degree.

By then, Frémont had found several influential friends. One of them helped him join an army surveying party working in the southern Appalachians—Cherokee country. After that, another got him a civilian appointment teaching mathematics to midshipmen aboard the USS *Natchez*. That job lasted two years. Each career step added to Frémont's resume. Finally, he received an appointment as a second lieutenant with the U.S. Army Corps of Topographical Engineers, an elite branch of the military. Formed in 1838, the Corps never had more than thirty-six officers, and these were very well qualified. Almost all of them had graduated near the top of their class at West Point.

Frémont was the exception. One of his benefactors, Joel Poinsett, became secretary of war and arranged for Frémont to join the Corps. The engineers' main responsibility was providing accurate maps for field commanders, and surveying routes for wagons and railroads. Many of the Corps' engineers also became famous explorers—and Frémont would be the most famous.

Frémont soon began moving up through the ranks. He joined a surveying expedition that traveled between the upper Mississippi and Missouri rivers. Well-known mapmaker Joseph Nicollet took Frémont under his wing and taught him mapping and much more. Frémont learned to make scientific observations of flora and fauna. He could soon take accurate celestial measurements when plotting his map positions. Later, he called the expedition his "Yale College and Harvard." With Nicollet's help, Frémont became an accomplished survey engineer. Frémont often shook his head at how absorbed his mentor was with science.

In 1839, Frémont visited Washington, D.C.. His friends and his position allowed him to move in society circles, and he fell in love with Jessie Benton, the teenaged daughter of the powerful senator Thomas Hart Benton of Missouri. The senator violently opposed the relationship. John and Jessie eloped on October 19, 1841. They eventually won over Jessie's father, and from that point on, Senator Benton vehemently supported Frémont's career.

JOHN C. FRÉMONT
Library of Congress, LC-USZ62-12910

In 1842, Benton found his first chance to help his son-in-law. The senator was a leading expansionist, with a strong belief in "Manifest Destiny." This doctrine held that the United States was destined to expand its borders and populate the western part of North America. To give destiny a hand, the expansionists pushed a thirty-thousand-dollar appropriation bill through the Senate; it funded a survey of the Oregon Trail, which would make it easier for emigrants to move to the Oregon Territory.

Joseph Nicollet was in poor health and could not lead the expedition. Senator Benton offered a suggestion: John C. Frémont. In the first of many instances, his father-in-law took an active role in promoting Frémont's career. Frémont strongly supported the expansionists. He realized that he could help Benton and his colleagues in return, if he took advantage of the opportunity.

The expedition set off in June of 1842. Frémont was accompanied by the German-born cartographer, topographer, and sketch artist Charles Preuss. Preuss became invaluable to Frémont's expeditions. Also on hand was Kit Carson, a former mountain man who Frémont met heading upstream from St. Louis on the steamboat *Rowena*. The encounter was fortunate. Carson told the young officer that he "had been some time in the mountains and thought (he) could guide him to any point he would wish to go." Impressed, Frémont offered Carson a job as guide at one hundred dollars a month. Carson accepted, and a lifelong friendship began.

Not many people had traveled the Oregon Trail, but the surveyors had no trouble with it. With Kit Carson leading the way, they reached central Colorado in July and headed for South Pass (in present-day Wyoming), touted by fur trapper Jedediah Smith years before as the best way to get to Oregon. All the while, the party took accurate measurements of the terrain and documented their observations of flora, fauna, and weather conditions. When, after traveling up the Sweetwater Valley, they reached the pass, Frémont was disappointed. He had pictured himself leading a band of explorers over a treacherous gap in the mountains. Instead, they approached the 7,550-foot pass from a gently sloping sandy saddle.

Frémont had orders to survey the route to this point and return home. But his nature rebelled against stopping so soon. He continued past the continental divide to the Wind River Range. There, among mountain ranges topped by spectacular peaks, he selected one that he proclaimed was the tallest and announced that he would climb it. The peak (called at various times Woodrow Wilson Peak and Frémont Peak) was not the tallest, but it served the purpose. In August 1842, after a difficult climb, Frémont planted an American flag on its 13,785-foot summit. The achievement was a grand one; it caught the public's eye and boosted Frémont's career.

The trip by rubber boat down the Platte River added to Frémont's reputation. The public saw only Frémont's adventurousness. Charles Preuss remembered the episode in another light: "It was certainly stupid of the young chief to be so foolhardy where the terrain was absolutely unknown."

When Frémont returned home, he worked with his wife, Jessie, to write a 207-page report of the expedition. The result was an extremely informative document. Intending to assist travelers heading west on the Oregon Trail, it mapped campsites, water holes, pasturage, and river crossings. It presented information on Native American tribes and western wildlife. The report was presented to Congress in 1843; the legislators authorized the printing of an unprecedented ten thousand copies.

Frémont's report was extremely popular in the United States. Even in Europe, potential immigrants read the Frémonts' flowery writing

FRÉMONT'S FIRST JOURNEYS WEST

about the wonders of the West with great interest. Frémont was only partly aware of the public acclaim. By the time the report was circulating, he had already headed west on another expedition.

This time, Frémont traveled to South Pass and beyond, into the Oregon Territory. Congress hoped the expedition would provide accurate surveys of the entire Oregon Trail. More, they wanted Frémont to connect his maps with maps made by Charles Wilkes—the naval explorer who had charted the Northwest's coastal bays and interior in 1841 and 1842—to form a whole. Once again, Frémont had a slightly different vision for his expedition.

In May of 1844, Frémont went to St. Louis and bought supplies for the expedition, including a mounted brass howitzer that fired twelve-pound cannonballs. The purpose of the cannon was never clear. In public, Frémont insisted that the weapon was necessary to ward off hostile Indians or maybe the British, who had claims on the Oregon Territory. The presence of the cannon implied to military leaders in Washington that the mission had a military nature, rather than a more peaceful scientific and mapmaking one.

The head of the Corps' topographical engineers ordered Frémont to leave the weapon behind, but his letter arrived too late—the expedition had already departed. Some suspected that Jessie Frémont purposely delayed forwarding the letter until her husband was beyond reach of the mails. In any case, Frémont wheeled, pulled, and pushed the cannon some three thousand miles across the continent. No one ever fired the cannon, except to practice on a herd of buffalo. But the adoring public now carried a mental picture of Frémont, the Pathfinder, crossing the wilds with a cannon in tow.

As before, Frémont did not blaze new trails to the West, but accurately mapped those that later became important for thousands of immigrants. Some settlers, inspired by the letters of Jedediah Smith and the writings of John C. Frémont, were already heading west. A party of fifty immigrants traveled alongside Frémont's troops for a while. The settlers' guide was the famous mountain man Joe Walker; he eventually took the wagon train all the way to California.

Another mountain man, Broken Hand Fitzgerald, guided Frémont's explorers. In Colorado, Kit Carson joined them and led the expedition to the Great Salt Lake of present-day Utah. Fur trapper Jim Bridger had discovered this inland salty sea; other mountain men had visited it; but no one had documented accurate details of the region. Frémont was impressed by the huge expanse of water, "stretching in still and solitary grandeur." He spent several days exploring its borders and mapping the terrain.

Returning to the Oregon Trail, the party crossed the Rockies and journeyed down the Snake and Columbia rivers. They followed the route Lewis and Clark had taken almost forty years earlier. Throughout their journey, the men plotted longitudes and latitudes. They estimated elevations using barometers, chronometers, field scopes, and other instruments that were carefully packed away during transport. Frémont and Preuss were the first to calculate the heights of Mount St. Helens, Mount Rainier, and Mount Hood. Previous travelers had suspected that these prominent peaks were volcanic. Frémont confirmed it. He witnessed an eruption of Mount St. Helens from fifty miles away.

In addition, the party collected hundreds of fossils, fish, birds, mammals, and—especially—plants. They found many species new to science, and one was later given the name *Fremontia vermicularis* after the expedition's leader.

On November 8, 1844, the party arrived at Fort Vancouver, their mission complete. Frémont sent a few men to the mouth of the Columbia River to formally link up with the lands that had been explored by Charles Wilkes. Then, once again, John Frémont set about reinterpreting his orders. The instructions told Frémont to return east after reaching Fort Vancouver. The Pathfinder did that, but by a different route. He made the return trip along some previously explored routes and some unexplored and quite dangerous routes. In so doing, he made himself a national hero.

In late November of 1844, Frémont left the Columbia River and headed south into California. And instead of taking the easy San Joaquin Valley route, Frémont led his party of thirty-seven men along the Sierra Nevada, the mounted howitzer still in tow. As countless later parties affirmed, the Sierras in winter are extremely inhospitable.

Frémont and his men entered the mountains in January. The weather was bitterly cold. By the time the group attempted to cross the High Sierra north of Lake Tahoe, the snow drifts were too deep to travel through. Many of the animals died from exposure and starvation. The men's conditions were not much better. They ate their dead horses to stay alive. The remaining animals were too weak to go on, and the men had to drag their gear up the snow-covered slopes. Two of the remaining horses slipped in the heavy snow and rolled some two hundred feet down the mountain. The explorers finally abandoned the cannon, after hauling it thousands of miles.

The situation became desperate. The men were trapped in uncharted mountains with only frostbite and starvation as prospects. Morale was low. Preuss, angry at the foolhardy crossing in winter, began referring to Frémont as "the Field Marshal." The Field Marshal, with the able assistance of the two guides, Carson and Fitzgerald, did finally get his men out. On January 26, 1845, Frémont led a party on snowshoes to open a way to the summit of the Sierras—a distance of ten miles. It took them eleven days, but they found a way out and came back for the others.

The weather ultimately saved them. The winter of 1844–1845 was actually relatively mild. In a normal year, they would all have perished, the expedition ending in disaster.

The entire party of emaciated explorers finally made it to Sutter's Fort along the western foothills of the Sierras. They rested for three weeks and purchased new animals and supplies. When they left, they picked up the Old Spanish Trail along the Mojave River and roughly retraced Jedediah Smith's old route through southern Nevada.

The men were now headed home, but more trials lay ahead. Several Indian tribes attacked or threatened them along the way. Eventually, they again met up with guide Joe Walker, who took them through a southern passage in the Rocky Mountains and on to more hospitable lands. Walker showed the Pathfinder some new shortcuts through the mountains, which Frémont duly surveyed and mapped.

In August of 1845, Frémont returned to Washington, D.C., triumphant. His expedition had covered twenty-five hundred miles. In just over fourteen months, he had made a broad circuit of the West. His expedition was the most important since Lewis and Clark's, and the American public eagerly awaited the printed accounts of the journey.

John and Jessie Frémont's second report was even more popular than the first. They made some noticeable errors, such as confusing the Great Salt Lake with Utah Lake, a freshwater lake. But, on balance, it was an extraordinary account and, again, Congress printed ten thousand copies.

Frémont's account challenged a long-held belief about the Great Plains. Previous explorer Major Stephen Long had called the Great Plains a bleak desert fit only for Indians. Frémont described it as a fertile region of ample grass and water, ripe for farming and raising livestock. He wrote, "In . . . the cultivation of grains and staple crops,

~ FREMONT'S EXPEDITION TO CALIFORNIA, 1845-1846

[the Great Plains] would be inferior to the Atlantic states, though many parts are superior for wheat, while in the flocks and herds it would claim a high place." No one realized that Frémont's visits to the area had coincided with years of high rainfall. The grasslands had appeared much more lush during his visits than they would in normal years.

Frémont also wrote about the Oregon Territory and California in glowing terms. His report convinced thousands of immigrants that the West was truly the promised land. The mass movement of people to the Great Plains and farther west in the 1840s, 1850s, and beyond was due, in no small part, to the efforts of John C. Frémont. His characterization of the Great Salt Lake region as a fertile garden spot convinced Brigham Young to lead his flock of Mormons to settle there. Others were drawn by his tales of fertile soil and timber in Oregon and California.

Frémont's most important contribution was the mapping he and Charles Preuss did. Their maps of the West did include many blank spots—Frémont refused to guess about areas that he himself had not explored, so he left them blank. The blank spots goaded him to explore even further.

Frémont got his next chance in the summer of 1845. Now a celebrity, Frémont was deluged with the applications of men wanting to join his next expedition. This time, he selected sixty men to survey the Arkansas and Red rivers and parts west. His exact orders are unclear; his third expedition, like the man himself, has a particular mystique. The survey party included artists, hunters, guides, mapmakers, and scientists. All the men in the party trained in marksmanship, which caused the Spanish in California to wonder about Frémont's true mission.

Frémont headed west and conducted his surveys as planned. But then he continued on to the Great Salt Lake and across the Great

Basin to the Sierra Nevada. At the eastern foot of the Sierras, the party split in two. Joe Walker took most of the men south, then west through Walker Pass and into the San Joaquin Valley. Frémont, Kit Carson, and fourteen men entered the mountains around present-day Donner Pass just before the first heavy snows of winter. This time, Frémont wasn't trapped by the snows and the two parties rejoined near San Jose in February of 1846.

From there, the expedition entered Monterey, which was well inside Spanish territory. Frémont asked the military governor, José Castro, for permission to make scientific observations. Castro at first granted the request, but then the Spaniards reconsidered and ordered the Americans out of California. Frémont refused to leave. He fortified his position atop Hawk's Peak, near the Salinas Valley. After some saber-rattling and bravado, Frémont withdrew northward, much to the anger of Joe Walker. The veteran mountain man called Frémont a coward and left the party.

Frémont may have had hidden motives for retreating all the way to southern Oregon. War was in the air. Frémont's party camped at Klamath Lake and waited. On June 8, 1846, Lieutenant Archibald Gillespie of the U.S. Marines arrived dressed in civilian clothes. Gillespie had traveled six hundred miles through great dangers to find Frémont. No one knows what Gillespie's message was, or whether Frémont knew that war had just been declared between the United States and Mexico.

Frémont's response to Gillespie's message was clear. He marched his men back to California. "Except for myself, then and for nine months afterward," he later wrote, "there was no other officer of the Army in California." Frémont traveled to the American River near Sacramento, where he joined forces with rebels calling themselves the Bear Flag Republic. He led his troop of ninety mounted men eighty miles to Sonoma, arriving on June 25, 1846. Frémont's men defeated some of Castro's troops in Sonoma and went on to capture Monterey as well.

The Americans achieved final victory in California. Frémont's small force swept down from the north; General Stephen Kearny's troops moved in from the east; and Commodore Richard Stockton's naval forces landed on the west. The Americans united in Los Angeles.

Here, John Frémont received a major lesson in politics. Commodore Stockton appointed Frémont the territorial governor. But General Kearny had his own nominee. He ordered Frémont to vacate California and disband his "California battalion." Frémont refused. He quickly learned that Kearny had more clout than did Stockton. John C. Frémont, national hero, Pathfinder, stalwart of the Mexican War, was taken back to Washington for court martial.

Frémont was charged with "mutiny, disobedience and conduct pre-judicial to military discipline." His brother-in-law defended him, but he was found guilty. The president allowed him to remain in the Army, but Frémont resigned on principle.

Most explorers would have settled into a life of retirement, but John Frémont was still energetic and still widely popular. No longer in the Army, Frémont had little trouble attracting investors and recruits for another expedition. Again, his father-in-law helped. Senator Benton had long wanted to build a transcontinental railroad westward from St. Louis. He hired Frémont to find and survey a practical route.

To reestablish himself in the public eye, Frémont vowed not only to survey the route, but to do so under the most extreme conditions, the better to demonstrate the value of Senator Benton's vision. He set off, reaching Bent's Fort, Colorado, on November 16, 1848. The

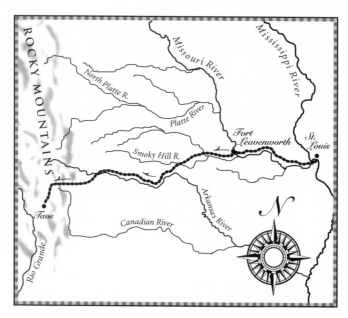

~ FRÉMONT'S SURVEY OF TRANSCONTINENTAL
RAILROAD ROUTE, 1848–1849

mountain men and guides there tried to dissuade the Pathfinder from
pressing on. Winter neared and conditions were already brutal. Also,
the fort had received reports that several Indian tribes were becoming unusually hostile.

Finally, Bill Williams agreed to guide the party. Williams was sixty-
two years old, but he had a world of experience. He had traveled the
mountains with Jedediah Smith, Joe Walker, Broken Hand Fitzgerald,
and many other legendary men. Williams recommended that the survey line head south from Pueblo. But Frémont would hear none of it.
He insisted they travel a straighter line, right through the Sangre de
Christo Mountains and into the San Juan Mountains.

By mid-December, the party was deep in the mountains and in
trouble. Ten feet of snow lay on the ground and temperatures reached

-20 degrees F. Nearly a hundred horses died. The men were suffering greatly. Most of the party had frostbitten noses and some had frozen hands and feet. As the last of their food ran out, they huddled together in the snow and awaited their fate. One by one, the starved men died, frozen in position by wind and snow.

The day after Christmas, 1848, Frémont sent Bill Williams and three men south toward New Mexico to try to reach one of the settlements and organize a rescue party. The remaining twenty-nine men stayed in the mountains and waited. No one came. One of the explorers, Ned Kern, wrote, "My food for four days consisted of the thigh of a (sage) hen that I cooked and recooked for breakfast and supper 8 times during those days."

Finally, on January 11, Frémont led four men on another desperate trek for help. They arrived at the headwaters of the Rio Grande River, at an elevation of eleven thousand feet, and the snow was still falling. A week of miserable struggle brought them no nearer to help. Climbing down the side of a ridge, they came upon a chilling scene. The original group of men, missing for over two weeks, huddled below them in the snow. One of the men, Henry King, was dead of exposure. Bill Williams and the other two men had barely survived— by eating their shoes, gun cases, and pack straps.

Together, the survivors of the two parties pressed on and eventually reached safety. They sent a rescue party back for the others, some of whom also survived. But, by the time the men arrived in Taos on January 27, 1849, most of them were suffering from snowblindness and frostbite. Ten men had died in the mountains.

The expedition had ended in disaster. Yet, later, when Frémont made his report on the proposed railroad route, he concluded, "The result was entirely satisfactory. It convinced me that neither snow of winter nor mountain ranges were obstacles in the way of a road."

That spring, Bill Williams and some of the other survivors returned to the San Juan Mountains to search for notes and equipment left behind during the flight to safety. The men were never seen again. It has long been assumed that Utes killed Williams and the others, but what really happened remains a mystery.

Frémont mounted one more expedition, his fifth. This, too, ended in tragedy. Attempting one more railroad survey along the 38th Parallel, he lost another man. Thus ended an incredible career of exploration.

But it was not the end of John C. Frémont. He served as a U.S. Senator from California, then became the presidential candidate for the newly formed Republican Party. Frémont's campaign slogan was "Free soil, free men, Frémont and victory." He promised to abolish slavery and do away with polygamy among the Mormons. Frémont did well in 1856, gaining 33 percent of the popular vote, with 45 percent of the vote in the North. But he lost the election to James Buchanan, 174 electoral votes to 114.

Frémont was touring Europe when the Civil War broke out. He returned immediately and was commissioned a major general—a significant career comeback for someone who had been court martialed less than twenty years earlier. The Pathfinder, still a prominent name in the public eye, had an undistinguished career in the Civil War. The army put him in charge of the Western Department, headquartered in St. Louis. But his tenure only lasted about a hundred days. After Frémont issued a proclamation confiscating the property—including slaves—of all rebels, President Abraham Lincoln relieved him of his command. Frémont was sent to western Virginia and put in charge of the Mountain Department.

In 1864, Frémont was again nominated for president, but he withdrew his name to promote the reelection of President Lincoln.

After the war, Frémont's career went through ups and downs. He had bought a seventy-square-mile ranch not far from Yosemite Valley for $3 thousand. Gold was discovered there, and Frémont became a rich man. He lost most of his wealth just as quickly in land speculations and other risky ventures. By the 1870s, he was penniless.

In 1878, Frémont was appointed Territorial Governor of Arizona at a salary of $2,600. He involved himself in more land deals, but these too ended badly. When his five-year term ended, Frémont was again destitute. He and Jessie moved to New York. In 1887, he worked with Jessie to write his memoirs. Frémont was working on a magazine article when he died in a Manhattan boardinghouse in 1890.

During Frémont's years of exploring and politics, Jessie had remained extremely loyal to her husband. Her writing skills helped make Frémont's expedition reports so popular. In addition to essentially writing her husband's memoirs, during the hard times of their later years, she supported the family with her writing. She regularly wrote and sold stories to *Harper's* and the New York *Ledger*, as well as other magazines and newspapers. She even wrote several books. After Frémont's death, she survived on a modest widow's pension, living in a house in Los Angeles that was donated by women of the city. When she died in 1902, her ashes were buried beside her husband's grave in New York.

Despite his nickname, the Pathfinder really explored few new areas of the West. But he did cover a huge portion of this barely-traveled country in his journeys, with the assistance of several capable guides. John Frémont's scientific contributions, especially his collections of new plants, are often overlooked. He was an experimenter too—he used an early version of a daguerreotype camera. Unfortunately, the camera was lost in the 1842 boating accident on the Platte River.

Frémont's main legacy was in his exceptionally skilled mapping of the lands that he covered. In many cases, his were the first accurate maps available. Along with his writings, the maps proved to be invaluable to waves of westward-bound immigrants. The most famous geographer of the day, Baron Alexander von Humboldt, personally congratulated Frémont on his achievements.

The congratulations were well deserved. With the possible exception of John Marshall, who one day stooped over and plucked a gold nugget from the ground at Sutter's Mill, no one individual encouraged the mass migration of people to the West more than John C. Frémont, the Pathfinder. ■

CHAPTER ELEVEN

~ *Down the Colorado*

John Wesley Powell

*B*y the end of the Civil War, most of the West had been explored. But no one had ever traveled the length of the Colorado River by water. The Colorado and its upstream tributaries, such as the Green and the Grand, passed through canyons that seemed to stretch to the sky. The rivers' waters were alternately brown from the loads of sediment it carried, and white from the series of violent, dangerous rapids along its course.

Jedediah Smith, James Ohio Pattie, Ewing Young, and other trappers and traders had crossed the river at various points and even traveled alongside it, but only high on the canyon rims. Few men dreamed of actually taming the Colorado and mapping its particular geology. More to the point, most people said such an attempt would be suicide. But John Wesley Powell wanted to row boats down the length of the Colorado River . . . and he only had one arm.

John Powell was a Civil War veteran. Born in 1834 in Palmyra, New York, he was the son of a poor farmer and part-time preacher. Later, the family moved to farms in Ohio and Wisconsin to scratch out a living from the soil. Powell never went to school in his youth; he studied at home. When he was eighteen, he passed an examination to become a school teacher. Earning a princely sum of fourteen dollars a month, Powell taught and learned alongside his students. He taught school in several towns in Illinois and briefly attended Wheaton, Illinois, and Oberlin colleges.

Along the way, Powell developed a keen interest in geology and natural history. During his summer vacations, the young teacher traveled through the Midwest, collecting rocks, plants, and fossils. In 1859, he was elected secretary of the Illinois Natural History Society. He had become an expert on mollusks and a curator of the Society's mollusk collection.

The outbreak of the Civil War cut short Powell's scientific studies. Twenty-seven years old, he enlisted as a private in the Twentieth Illinois. Powell was a born leader. In the early days of the war, the troops customarily elected their own officers and sergeants. Powell rapidly rose to sergeant. Just before the troops saw their first action, he became a second lieutenant; within a few months, he was promoted to artillery captain and thrust into one of the bloodiest battles of the war—Shiloh. In the heat of battle, Powell put up his hand to signal the firing of his artillery battery; he was hit in his right arm. The shattered arm was amputated on April 8, 1862.

Captain Powell's Civil War career continued despite the loss of his arm. He helped construct roads and bridges in the South. In 1864, just before the battle of Vicksburg, Powell was promoted to major.

But when the war ended, Powell was unemployed—a one-armed ex-soldier had few prospects. The soldier's home state had followed his wartime exploits, however, and was aware of his practical knowledge. Illinois Wesleyan University offered the major a position as professor of geology, with an attractive salary of a thousand dollars a year.

Powell loved geology, and he took the opportunity to develop the budding naturalist in himself too. He led his students on numerous field trips to study zoology, botany, and paleontology, as well as geology. Having only one arm was an inconvenience, but not a hindrance.

Despite these pleasant times, Powell soon tired of the comparatively slow pace in Illinois. Several notable explorers—among them Ferdinand Hayden, Clarence King, and George Wheeler—had led great surveying expeditions across the western territories. Their achievements combined science and cartography; they were exploring the last unmapped regions of the West. Powell wanted to play a part in these exciting times.

With none of the contacts or financial backing of the other great explorers of the day, Powell managed to convince the War Department and the Smithsonian Institution to provide him with some equipment to venture into the Southwest. Most of the money that financed the expedition he raised himself—he received small grants from several colleges. In 1867, Powell set off on his first expedition with ten others, including his wife Emma.

The party climbed Pikes Peak, then headed into the high mountains of Colorado. Eventually, they came to the headwaters of the Grand River, the upstream section of the Colorado River.

Although the Colorado had been discovered decades before, little was known of its lower reaches. Fur trappers Sylvester and James Pattie had been the first white men to see the immense Grand Canyon of the Colorado from its rim. Huge rapids had kept most explorers from venturing down the great river itself. A few adventuresome types had peered over the sides of the river's many canyons—some over five thousand feet deep. But the steep sides and long drops of these canyons and the huge quantities of river water that would swamp most boats humbled their ambitions.

The Colorado fascinated Powell. As a geologist, he could think of few more interesting places. Over millions of years, the river had etched its way through layer after layer of rock, exposing the history of the Earth along its canyon walls.

After asking around about what lay south of Colorado's mountains, Powell and his companions made plans for an expedition down the Grand River, which joined the Green River to form the Colorado. In 1868, funded by a number of government agencies, railroads, and colleges, Powell launched one more scouting trip to the upper reaches of the river. With great energy, the party clambered up huge mountains and explored high valleys. They were the first to climb Longs Peak, a majestic 14,255-foot mountain discovered but not scaled by members of Stephen Long's expedition almost fifty years earlier. Powell collected rocks, plants, and animals from the area around Grand Lake, the origin of the Colorado River.

To add to his own impressions of the Colorado's tributaries, Powell sought information from others. He talked with Native Americans who had traveled in the area and with the Mormons, who had established several settlements there. He talked with the mountain men who had meandered through the country for decades. Everyone had pieces of information on what he might expect, but no one knew the whole picture. Seeing the greater view would take a man with sand—a man like John Wesley Powell.

Over the next few months, Powell sought backers for his great expedition down the Colorado. In May of 1869, everything was ready. Two Illinois colleges had pledged funds; Powell had invested most of his own savings in the trip; the War Department and the Smithsonian Institute assisted with supplies and scientific instruments; and the railroads offered to transport the supplies westward.

On the afternoon of May 24, 1869, Powell and nine fellow

JOHN WESLEY POWELL

USGS Photographic Library

adventurers—including the major's brother, Walter—launched four wooden boats down the Green River. They intended to travel eight hundred to a thousand miles downstream, first on the Green River, then on the Colorado itself. Thus began one of the last great expeditions of discovery in the West—and one of the most difficult ever undertaken.

Powell had designed the boats himself. Three of them were twenty-one-foot-long oak craft, with double ribs for strength. The fourth was only sixteen feet long and made of pine, with places for storing food and equipment. The men named each of the boats. The smallest, the *Emma Dean*, took the lead when they left the tiny town of Green River City in southern Wyoming. They carried provisions to last ten months, including heavy clothing in case they were still on the river when winter arrived.

Besides traveling the length of the country's last unexplored river, Powell planned to keep a detailed journal of the trip and make scientific measurements as he went. He was as interested in the geology of the land as anything else. During the trip, he was constantly on the lookout for specimens of rocks and fossils.

The rivers—first the Green, then the Colorado—had many surprises in store for the travelers. On only the second day of the trip, three of the boats ran aground on a sand bar. By the time they dragged their vessels free, the men were thoroughly drenched. Then, after a few days of relatively easy drifting, they entered the first of many deep canyons. This one they named Flaming Gorge after Powell's description of it as a "flaming brilliant red gorge." It was deep and dark and full of foaming rapids. The wild water carried them through three immense canyons in only an hour—just a taste of things to come.

Every bend of the river brought wondrous sights. They passed a huge, beehive-shaped nest of swallows. Later, they saw the words

"Ashley 1825" carved into a rock, probably inscribed by a member of the Ashley Expedition—an attempt to tame the Colorado that had ended in failure. The river's rapids were sometimes so violent that the men had to lower the vessels downstream with long ropes. In many places, the rapids turned to waterfalls that tossed the boats around like corks.

Throughout the first few weeks, the men had plenty to eat. They shot grouse, deer, and even a mountain sheep. Not far downstream from Green River City, they had stopped at a hidden cave to retrieve some supplies that Powell had cached during his 1868 scouting trip. As the trip progressed and the canyons walls became steeper, the men saw fewer animals; they had to rely more on the supplies they carried in their boats.

On June 8, the party reached the Canyon of Lodore. Powell wrote that it "opened like a beautiful portal to a region of glory." With anticipation and more than a little fear, the men entered the huge canyon. They could hear the roar of the rapids; they could see the mist rising above the surface of the water where it plunged downward, out of sight. It would be the worst stretch of rapids they had yet encountered.

Powell's diary describes how the river dropped ten feet in some places, twenty feet in others. The sturdy but tiny boats swirled through the rapids and over the falls. Time and time again, huge waves drenched the men and their equipment. The oarsmen worked to keep the boats heading downstream and away from rocks and canyon walls; the others frantically bailed water.

Then one of the boats—the *No Name*—plunging through the rapids half-filled with water, crashed into some rocks. The oak sides crumbled and the three men inside were thrown into the swirling waters. All of them made it to a small sand shoal. The waters tumbled

~ Powell's exploration of the Colorado
River and its Tributaries, 1869.

around them, dragging at their legs. In a daring maneuver, one of the other boats came to their rescue.

The men were saved, but the boat and two thousand pounds of supplies were lost—clothes, food, guns, ammunition, and cooking gear. The ten adventurers squeezed into the three remaining boats.

The following morning, two of the men managed to retrieve barometers, thermometers, and a keg of whiskey from the wreck of the *No Name*. The party decided to portage around what remained of the series of rapids, rather than chancing the loss of more boats. Powell named the steep rapids "Disaster Falls" because of the loss of so much valuable equipment and food. For four long days, they worked at bypassing the small stretch of river. All the supplies had to be hand-carried to a point well past the rapids. The men then dragged and lowered each boat downstream, inching them past the rocks and through the treacherous waves. On the fifth day, they were able to journey by water again.

Day after day, they traveled through the Canyon of Lodore, traversing one set of rapids after another. Finally, the river widened as the Yampa, the last great tributary, entered the Colorado. Downstream, the expedition entered a great valley full of wild game. The men camped there to regain their strength. Farther on, they might not find fresh meat.

The party had been traveling for a month. Each day had presented more hardships than the one before. All the men had cuts and bruises, and every piece of clothing was soaking wet. It was a good time to rest. Some of the men caught trout from the river, and others hunted for deer and ducks. The explorers filled their stomachs with wild berries.

Powell and some of the men hiked inland to the Uinta Indian Agency in northern Utah, a distance of almost thirty miles. There, they obtained enough flour to last (they hoped) for the rest of the trip. Also at the agency, the men mailed letters. It was fortunate that they did. The eastern newspapers had widely proclaimed that all the members of the Powell Expedition were drowned. Many newspapers now printed the entire contents of the letters to disprove the earlier news and as evidence of the expedition's progress.

Frank Goodman, one of the men who hiked to the Indian station, decided not to return to the river. He had been thrown into the river when the No Name broke apart, and he had had enough adventuring to last a lifetime. Powell consented to his request; Goodman had been a valuable member of the team, but the boats were overloaded. Goodman's departure for home would leave nine voyagers. They had spent five weeks traveling three hundred river miles—and they had a longer, even more difficult journey ahead of them.

The days passed on the river, mile after mile, bend after bend.

Each day seemed to run into the next. Occasionally, an event worth recording occurred. On July 6, most of the men became violently ill after eating a meal of roots and vegetables from an abandoned garden. A white hunter and his Indian wife had planted the garden—the man had previously invited Powell to stop and take what he needed. One of the explorers suggested that the tops of potato plants were good greens. After several hours of nausea, vomiting, and severe stomach pain, one of the expedition's members, Jack Summer, wrote in his diary, "potato tops are not good for greens on the 6th day of July."

One day, Powell almost fell while climbing a cliff. One of the party, George Bradley, rescued the one-armed major, lowering a pair of long johns to him to use as a rope. Unperturbed, Powell wrote that they proceeded to "make the necessary observations for determining its (the top of the canyon) altitude above the camp." Another day, waves swamped one of the boats in a stretch of river the men named the Canyon of Desolation. Guns, pieces of scientific equipment, and oars were swept away, lost. The men's spirits sank further. Only Major Powell now greeted every day with energy, and an eagerness to see what adventures they would meet around the next turn of the river.

In mid-July, the boats entered a region of high desert. Wildlife was scarce. The water moved slowly, and the men had to row to make any headway. After a long, desolate period, the expedition reached the mouth of the Grand River—the other major arm of the Colorado. The explorers took another welcome week of rest, heading downstream again on July 21. They had traveled 375 winding miles.

Now the river was even more powerful than before. The party had come to the main stem of the Colorado, their ultimate objective. It was virgin river—no one had ever traveled it. No maps existed, nor did rumors of what might await the voyagers. The men were plunging headlong into the unknown. Happy to be moving again, they still felt some trepidation at the thought of the probabilities ahead: life-threatening rapids, impassable waterfalls in canyons too high to scale, and hostile Indians.

On the very first day on the Colorado, the party ran into difficult rapids, and one of the boats was swamped. The men lost more supplies to the river. Alternate searing heat and drenching water had already ruined much of the food; with this second capsize, stores were miserably low. A week later, however, the explorers managed to shoot two desert sheep. The fresh meat was a welcome addition to their diet.

The days had a sameness about them for a while. The travelers rowed through quiet stretches of the river, portaged around difficult rapids, and challenged other stretches of whitewater. Major Powell and his men took scientific measurements and carefully mapped each bend in the river, every canyon and geological feature.

But Powell had started to worry about the river itself. He had predicted that the rapids would become easier once the party entered the main trunk of the Colorado. The gradient—the drop in the river's altitude—would be more gradual, he thought, so the pace would slow, making the traveling safer. But the river was proving him wrong. Mile by mile, the rapids were getting worse. Almost every day they had to choose: they could waste precious time and food supplies in lengthy portages, or they could risk destroying their boats and drowning in the process.

As August began, morale reached a new low. The food was almost gone; the men had to ration what little they had. Their clothes and boots were tattered. One day, they chanced upon some abandoned pueblos. Perhaps the first humans to see the ruins in hundreds of years, the explorers were too exhausted to realize the significance of their discovery.

The men had now been traveling for ten weeks, without seeming to get any closer to the journey's end. They were hot, hungry, and physically drained. Each day brought another small tragedy. A box of soda was lost, so they couldn't bake bread. Their last sack of flour broke loose and dropped to the bottom of the river.

At long last, they entered the Grand Canyon. For a geologist, it was the most fascinating wonder of creation. Powell wrote page after page in his journal, describing the unique geological features of the 217-mile-long gorge. "The wonders of the Grand Canyon cannot be adequately represented in symbols of speech nor by speech itself," he wrote. "The elements that unite to make the Grand Canyon the most sublime spectacle in nature are multifarious and exceedingly diverse." He drew dozens of sketches in an attempt to convey what he saw.

The beauty of the canyon was not lost on the other men, but most of them couldn't enjoy it. They merely continued on. Somehow, the nine men found a source of inner strength—enough to keep rowing, pulling on ropes at portages, and faithfully recording scientific measurements.

On August 14, their food almost gone, the party encountered a small band of Native Americans. They traded for some melons and vegetables—the most delicious treat the travelers could imagine. The excitement didn't last long. Almost before the meal was digested, the river turned to the west; the three boats entered perhaps the most dangerous stretch of rapids ever charted. The whitewater went on for miles. Bend after bend, the men maneuvered the tiny boats around rocks and away from giant standing waves. Portaging wasn't an option; the steep canyon walls left no banks and few footholds.

Such strenuous work after three months of hardship and deprivation thoroughly exhausted the men. Three of them decided to quit the expedition. O. G. Howland, his brother Seneca, and hunter-trapper William Dunn asked Powell for permission to quit—to climb out of the canyon and return home. The major hated to see his compatriots leave, but he understood. The men had endured more than most humans could have borne.

On August 28, the three men left, carrying two rifles and a shotgun. They refused to take any of the meager rations, but the cook snuck them some freshly baked biscuits. The others watched them climb up a side canyon to reach the desert floor. In O. G. Howland's pocket was a letter from Powell to his wife, Emma. Another man gave Howland his pocket watch to give to the man's sister. Those left behind felt bereft; they saw their chances of success slipping away.

Only six explorers remained—not enough to man all three boats. Powell abandoned the smallest craft, the *Emma Dean* near what is known as Separation Rapids. The party pressed on, traversing one incredible set of rapids after another. Then, on August 29, without warning, the rapids disappeared. The river was quiet. It took some time for the travelers to realize they had made it. They had become the first to explore the length of the mighty Colorado River.

Soon after the rapids passed from view, the river emerged from its canyons and meandered through a broad desert. A group of Mormons lived next to the river in a little town called Callville, near the mouth of the Virgin River. Three men and a boy were fishing, and others were working in their gardens; they looked up and were greatly surprised to see a ragtag group of men emerge from the upstream canyon.

Much later, the major learned the fate of the three men who had left the expedition less than two days before it ended. They had traded the perils of the river for danger of another kind. When they reached the top of the canyon, all three were killed by Indians.

Powell learned the news from some Shivwit Indians who mentioned having killed three white men. The three had stumbled into the Shivwit village, starving and exhausted. The Indians mistook them for some white miners who had killed a tribal woman during a drunken incident. Believing that no other white men could possibly be in the area, the Shivwits chased the men down and killed them. Powell despaired at hearing the news, but he understood how the tragedy had happened. The actions of irresponsible white men had resulted in the deaths of three innocent travelers.

News of the expedition's success reached the populated centers of the country. John Wesley Powell was an instant celebrity. Most people had long ago given him up for dead. But Powell and his five fellow adventurers proved that sheer determination can overcome the toughest of obstacles.

Powell's trip down the Colorado was no fluke. It was the indulgence of a life's passion: Powell truly loved the desert land. In 1871, he made the trip again, this time with a $12 thousand government appropriation. He improved his maps and named the previously unexplored region the Colorado Plateau. Even then, he wasn't finished; he sponsored more expeditions to the region and wrote several books. One of them, *A Report Upon Lands of the Arid Regions of the United States*, has been called one of the first books on wilderness preservation. Almost lost in its wealth of geological information is an abundance of information on Southwestern Indian basketry, language, and customs.

Powell continued to work in the field until 1875, when he became an administrator in Washington, D.C. In 1879, he helped establish the United States Geological Survey. Powell had come full circle. His intense interest in geology led him to explore the Colorado Plateau, containing perhaps the most marvelous geological features in North America. And his explorations prompted him to establish a framework so that others could continue studying his beloved land.

Powell later headed the U.S. Geological Survey for thirteen years. He died in 1902, at the age of sixty-eight.

On his first trip down the Colorado River, John Wesley Powell had spent many evenings hiking alone through uncharted canyons. Sometimes, he sat on a canyon rim with the river meandering far below, following its own hundreds-of-miles-long journey to the sea. As he sat there, the sleeve of his missing arm flapping in the evening breeze, names came to his mind: Lewis and Clark, Manuel Lisa, Zebulon Pike, Jedediah Smith . . . all the courageous explorers who had gone before him.

Perhaps Powell even dreamed of himself as a member of that exclusive group. He had every right to. The era of the great western explorers was nearing its close, and John Wesley Powell would be remembered as one of those giants: the men with sand. ■

Suggested Reading

General Works:

Cleland, Robert Glass. *This Reckless Breed of Men*. Albuquerque: University of New Mexico Press, 1950.

Dary, David. *Entrepreneurs of the Old West*. New York: Alfred A. Knopf, 1986.

Gilbert, Bil. *The Trailblazers*. New York: Time-Life Books, 1973.

Goetzmann, William H. *Exploring the American West, 1803–1879*. Washington, D.C.: National Park Service, 1982.

———. *New Lands, New Men*. New York: Viking, 1986.

Sandoz, Mari. *The Beaver Men*. New York: Hastings House, 1964.

Van Orman, Richard A. *The Explorers: Nineteenth Century Expeditions in Africa and the American West*. Albuquerque: University of New Mexico Press, 1984.

Viola, Herman J. *Exploring the West*. Washington, D.C.: Smithsonian Books, 1987.

John Colter:

Harris, Burton. *John Colter, His Years in the Rockies*. New York: Scribner, 1952.

Meriwether Lewis and William Clark:

Allen, John Logan. *Lewis and Clark and the Image of the American Northwest*. New York: Dover, 1975.

Ambrose, Stephen E. *Undaunted Courage*. New York: Simon and Schuster, 1996.

Bakeless, John (Editor). *The Journals of Lewis and Clark*. New York: The New American Library, 1964.

Bergon, Frank (Editor). *The Journals of Lewis and Clark*. New York: Penguin Books, 1989.

Coues, Elliott (Editor). *The History of the Lewis and Clark Expedition*. 3 Vols. New York: Dover, 1893.

Cutright, Paul Russell. *Lewis and Clark: Pioneering Naturalists*. Lincoln: University of Nebraska Press, 1989.

DeVoto, Bernard (Editor). *The Journals of Lewis and Clark.* Boston: Houghton-Mifflin Company, 1953.

Dillon, Richard. *Meriwether Lewis.* New York: Coward-McCann, 1965.

Furtwangler, Albert. *Acts of Discovery.* Urbana: University of Illinois, 1993.

Lavender, David. *The Way to the Western Sea.* New York: Doubleday, Anchor Books, 1988.

John C. Frémont:

Jackson, Donald, and Mary Lee Spence (Editors). *The Expeditions of John Charles Frémont.* 3 vols., plus maps. Urbana: University of Illinois Press, 1970.

Preuss, Charles. *Exploring With Frémont.* Translated and edited by Erwin G. and Elisabeth K. Gudde. Norman: University of Oklahoma Press, 1958.

Richmond, Patricia Joy. *Trail to Disaster.* Niwot, Colorado: University Press of Colorado, 1990.

Manuel Lisa:

Oglesby, Richard Edward. *Manuel Lisa and the Opening of the Missouri Fur Trade.* Norman: University of Oklahoma Press, 1963.

Stephen Long:

Evans, Howard Ensign. *The Natural History of the Long Expedition to the Rocky Mountains, 1819–1820.* New York: Oxford University Press, 1997.

Goodman, George J., and Cheryl A. Lawson. *Retracing Major Stephen H. Long's 1820 Expedition.* Norman: University of Oklahoma Press, 1995.

James, Edwin. *Account of an Expedition from Pittsburgh to the Rocky Mountains.* Barre, Massachusetts: The Imprint Society, 1972.

Nichols, Roger L., and Patrick L. Halley. *Stephen Long and American Frontier Exploration.* Norman: University of Oklahoma Press, 1995.

Alexander Mackenzie:

Bryce, George. *The Makers of Canada: Mackenzie, Selkirk, Simpson.* Toronto: Morang and Company, 1906.

Mackenzie, Alexander. *Alexander Mackenzie's Voyage to the Pacific Ocean in 1793.* New York: The Citadel Press, 1967.

Mackenzie, Alexander. *Voyages From Montreal Through the Continent of North America to the Frozen and Pacific Oceans in 1789 and 1793.* 2 vols. New York: Allerton Book Company, 1922.

Mirsky, Jeannette. *The Westward Crossings.* New York: Alfred A. Knopf, 1946.

Sheppe, Walter (Editor). *First Man West*. Berkeley: University of California Press, 1962.

Woollacott, Arthur. *Mackenzie and His Voyageurs*. London: J.M. Dent and Sons, 1927.

Sylvester and James Pattie:

Batman, Richard. *James Pattie's West*. Norman: University of Oklahoma Press, 1986.

Pattie, James O. *The Personal Narrative of James O. Pattie, of Kentucky*. Cincinnati: E.H. Flint, 1833. There are several reprinted versions of this original work.

Zebulon Pike:

Hollon, W. Eugene. *Lost Pathfinder: Zebulon Montgomery Pike*. Norman, University of Oklahoma Press, 1949.

Jackson, David (Editor). *The Journals of Zebulon Montgomery Pike*. 2 vols. Norman: University of Oklahoma Press, 1966.

Terrell, John Upton. *Zebulon Pike: The Life and Times of the Adventurer*. New York: Weybright and Talley, 1968.

John Wesley Powell:

Bartlett, Richard A. *Great Surveys of the American West*. Norman: University of Oklahoma Press, 1962.

Dellenbaugh, Frederick S. *A Canyon Voyage: The Narrative of the Second Powell Expedition*. Tucson: University of Arizona Press, 1908.

Powell, J.W. *The Exploration of the Colorado River and its Canyons*. New York: Dover, 1961 (originally published in 1895 as *Canyons of the Colorado* by Flood and Vincent).

Jedediah Smith:

Morgan, Dale L. *Jedediah Smith and the Opening of the West*. Lincoln: University of Nebraska Press, 1953.

Charles Wilkes:

Schmucker, Samuel M. *The Life of Dr. Elisha Kent Kane and of Other Distinguished American Explorers*. Philadelphia: John E. Potter and Company, 1858.

Wilkes, Charles. *Narrative of the United States Exploring Expedition, During the Years 1838, 1839, 1840, 1841, 1842*. In 5 vols. Philadelphia, 1845.

Index

About the Author

John Moring is a professor of Zoology at the University of Maine and the author of more than 125 articles in scientific journals and more than 50 popular articles and short stories in national and regional magazines. For more than 20 years, he has been researching aspects of western history and is a member of the Western History Association, Western Writers of America, Mining History Association, and other organizations. He is the author of the book, *Arthur Hill: Western Actor, Miner, and Law Officer,* as well as western history articles in *Old West, True West, Persimmon Hill, Journal of the West,* and other publications.